1,000,000 Books

are available to read at

www.ForgottenBooks.com

Read online
Download PDF
Purchase in print

ISBN 978-0-365-51933-1
PIBN 11262091

This book is a reproduction of an important historical work. Forgotten Books uses state-of-the-art technology to digitally reconstruct the work, preserving the original format whilst repairing imperfections present in the aged copy. In rare cases, an imperfection in the original, such as a blemish or missing page, may be replicated in our edition. We do, however, repair the vast majority of imperfections successfully; any imperfections that remain are intentionally left to preserve the state of such historical works.

Forgotten Books is a registered trademark of FB &c Ltd.
Copyright © 2018 FB &c Ltd.
FB &c Ltd, Dalton House, 60 Windsor Avenue, London, SW19 2RR.
Company number 08720141. Registered in England and Wales.

For support please visit www.forgottenbooks.com

1 MONTH OF FREE READING

at

www.ForgottenBooks.com

By purchasing this book you are eligible for one month membership to ForgottenBooks.com, giving you unlimited access to our entire collection of over 1,000,000 titles via our web site and mobile apps.

To claim your free month visit:

www.forgottenbooks.com/free1262091

* Offer is valid for 45 days from date of purchase. Terms and conditions apply.

English
Français
Deutsche
Italiano
Español
Português

www.forgottenbooks.com

Mythology Photography **Fiction**
Fishing Christianity **Art** Cooking
Essays Buddhism Freemasonry
Medicine **Biology** Music **Ancient Egypt** Evolution Carpentry Physics
Dance Geology **Mathematics** Fitness
Shakespeare **Folklore** Yoga Marketing
Confidence Immortality Biographies
Poetry **Psychology** Witchcraft
Electronics Chemistry History **Law**
Accounting **Philosophy** Anthropology
Alchemy Drama Quantum Mechanics
Atheism Sexual Health **Ancient History**
Entrepreneurship Languages Sport
Paleontology Needlework Islam
Metaphysics Investment Archaeology
Parenting Statistics Criminology
Motivational

HOW THE WAR BEGAN IN 1914

BEING THE DIARY OF THE RUSSIAN FOREIGN OFFICE FROM THE 3rd TO THE 20th (Old Style) OF JULY, 1914

Published by the "Red Archives" Department of the Russian Soviet Government in their "Historical Journal" Vol. IV 1923.

Translated from the Original Russian by
MAJOR W. CYPRIAN BRIDGE

WITH A FOREWORD TO THE TRANSLATION BY
S. D. SAZONOV, G.C.B., G.C.V.O.
Late Russian Minister for Foreign Affairs

AND

AN INTRODUCTION BY
BARON M. F. SCHILLING, C.V.O.

LONDON: GEORGE ALLEN & UNWIN LTD.
RUSKIN HOUSE, 40 MUSEUM STREET, W.C.1

First published in 1925

Printed in Great Britain by
UNWIN BROTHERS, LIMITED, LONDON AND WOKING

(All rights reserved)

FOREWORD

The diary of the chief of my diplomatic Chancellery relating to the period preceding the Great War published by the Bolsheviks in the hope of discovering fresh material for the renewal of their anti-Russian propaganda, and which has been lately translated into German, is being now published in English for the convenience of Anglo-Saxon readers.

I, for my part, can but welcome this initiative, feeling assured that any impartial reader who is acquainted with the official documents concerning these fateful days will not fail to take interest in the brief records of Baron Schilling.

Their value consists chiefly in their absolutely private character, which excluded any possibility of their being published. They were often jotted down in haste, but always from direct sources of information and under the influence of the rapid development of events, and it would seem, consequently, difficult to doubt their veracity.

Nevertheless, a group of German political men, including M. von Jagow, Count Pourtalès and some others, who have made it their object to remove the burden of responsibility from the German Government by all means in their power, and to transfer it to the shoulders of Lord Grey, M. Poincaré, M. Isvolsky and myself, has seized upon this diary, in which they have contrived to find proofs not merely of malignity but even of forgery.

I have not the slightest intention of beginning a controversy with M. von Jagow and Count Pourtalès, all the more so as the bad taste which characterizes their attacks on Baron Schilling and myself makes me most unwilling to enter into a detailed discussion of the matter.[1]

In consequence of this, my intention is to address myself in this short preface to those who are capable of forming an impartial opinion of recent events. Such persons are, fortunately, to be found not only in Europe and America, but even in Germany itself. The proof of this assertion we find in the persistency and violence with which M. von Jagow, Count Pourtalès, Baron Romberg, M. Delbruck, etc., etc., carry on their campaign. It is clearly evident that their philippics are intended for home consumption, as it is hardly possible to assume that they hope to alter in their favour the opinion of foreigners, based on an accurate knowledge of official documents and chiefly the German ones, which throw a vivid light upon the Austro-German plans and dispositions during the eventful summer of 1914.

Now that all the holes and corners of our archives have been ransacked, and all their hidden documents have been published, it is hardly possible to say anything new about the events which preceded the European war.

I therefore intend to mention only the most salient moments of this tragic period. I shall, of course, speak from the point of view of the Russian Government, without touching on the actions of its former allies and friends, whose sincerity and straightforwardness have been sufficiently demonstrated by their own authoritative politicians.

[1] *Die Kriegsschuldfrage,* September 1924.

Russia is accused of having entertained ambitious designs against the security and welfare of Europe as early as the Reval interview between the Emperor Nicholas II and King Edward VII, while at the same time her accusers are oblivious of the fact that another interview had likewise taken place at Bjerkö between the Emperors of Russia and Germany. Although this last interview must be considered as a manifestation on the part of Russia of political sentimentality devoid of any practical significance, it was in no sense hostile to Germany.

As regards the preparations she was also accused of entertaining in view of a war with Germany, one cannot help being reminded of the fable of the wolf and the lamb.

While on the one hand Germany was prepared in every respect for war, and especially so from the point of view of strategical railways, Russia, on the other, was pitifully and hopelessly backward in every way, which, however, does not deter certain German writers from asserting that Russia's belated attempts to develop her net of strategical railways were a menace to Germany.

What were the attitudes of the St. Petersburg and the allied Austrian and German Cabinets during the Austro-Serbian conflict?

While in the name of the Russian Government five propositions were made equally conciliatory, reaching as far as the withdrawal of Russia from the discussion of the conflict and the undertaking immediately to suspend all warlike preparations without any corresponding engagement on the part of Austria, M. von Jagow, acting the part of the custodian of the Habsburg Monarchy, refused any discussion of the Russian propositions, which he rejected as being unacceptable to Austria-Hungary.

Everyone must be allowed to form his own opinion as to the motives which prompted Germany in refusing to bring some mitigation on her part to the acuteness of a conflict which threatened the peace of Europe.

Whether Germany actually desired war, as some suppose, in order to establish once for all her hegemony over continental Europe, or whether, as others think, she hoped by using intimidation, as she had succeeded in doing before in similar circumstances, to bring to a successful issue Austria's insane venture, I leave to others to decide.

In any case, even taking into consideration the peculiarities of German psychology, it is hardly possible to admit that M. von Jagow and his chief could really expect to persuade Russia that Austria's designs against Serbia, the object of which, as we now know, was the destruction of that country's independence, and consequently the actual overthrow of the Balkan *statu quo* to the advantage of Austria and Germany and the detriment of Russia, could be considered as a question not concerning international politics, but as one of merely local interest. It should be here remembered that, at that time, Constantinople and the Straits, owing to the occupation by General Liman-Sanders and his numerous staff of most of the responsible military posts in Turkey, were virtually in the hands of Germany, and that consequently the whole of the Balkan Peninsula was on the point of being absorbed by the two Central Empires.

As regards the advice given by the Russian Government to Serbia, it likewise was characterized by an equally conciliatory spirit. Its object was to induce Serbia to accept all the clauses of the Austrian ultimatum excepting those which encroached upon the sovereign rights of Serbia. It is to the lasting honour of the Serbian statesmen that this advice was accepted.

Is there, then, any indication to suppose that such judicious advice was proffered by Germany to her Austrian ally? M. von Jagow, while assuring the Entente Powers that he was exerting a moderating influence in Vienna, gave opposite instructions to the German Ambassador in his confidential correspondence with him.

Referring to the question of the Russian mobilization, to which German writers attach such importance, stated briefly the facts which preceded it or coincided with it were as follows: (1) On the 30th of July the Russian mobilization was decided upon about five o'clock p.m., and proclaimed on the 31st, after Belgrade had been bombarded by the Austrians; (2) Austria's mobilization was in full swing; (3) the semi-official *Local Anzeiger* had published in a special edition the decree of the German mobilization, which was afterwards denied, but not before it had time to reach St. Petersburg;[1] (4) Count Pourtalès had, on the 29th, in the name of his Government, presented the demand that Russia should stop all military preparations on her western frontiers without any reciprocal undertaking on the part of Austria; (5) the Emperor Nicholas had proposed to the Kaiser to submit the Austro-Serbian conflict to The Hague Tribunal; (6) the

[1] See Kautzky, *Deutsche Dokumente zum Kriegsausbruch*, iii, 488, p. 7. Also published in English by the Carnegie Endowment for International Peace, *Outbreak of the World War*, German Documents collected by Karl Kautsky, New York, 1924, No. 488, p. 403: "I do not consider it impossible that the Russian mobilization can be traced to rumours rife here yesterday—absolutely false and at once officially denied, but which were reported at Petersburg as fact—that mobilization was taking place here.—BETHMANN-HOLLWEG."

" Kriegsgefahrzustand," which is equivalent to a decree of mobilization in any other country, " mobilization " being inseparable in Germany, according to Count Pourtalès, with the commencement of hostilities, had been announced in Berlin on the 31st of July, i.e. simultaneously with the announcement of the Russian mobilization.

I conclude these brief introductory lines by mentioning the accusation often addressed by Germany to France and Russia, that they desired war in order that France might recover her lost provinces and Russia acquire the Straits and Constantinople.

As regards the latter, I feel bound to state that shortly after Germany had declared war upon the Dual Alliance, and before the Berlin Government had sent its warships through the Straits into the Black Sea and had thus drawn Turkey into a war with Russia, the Russian Government, together with its Allies, had offered Turkey to guarantee her territorial integrity on the sole condition of her remaining neutral.

This fact, officially announced in the Russian Orange Book, speaks for itself, putting an end to the accusations piled up in Berlin against Russian diplomacy.

SAZONOV.

INTRODUCTION

THE origin of the "Diary of the Former Ministry for Foreign Affairs," published in the *Red Archives* (vol. iv, Moscow, 1923), and now reproduced in an English translation, was as follows :—

Knowing from experience that official documents preserved in the archives only contain in the majority of cases the records of the outcome of deliberations and conversations which of themselves will elude the inquiring eyes of the future historian, I endeavoured throughout the period of my diplomatic service to set down the circumstances, sometimes trifling but not devoid of a certain measure of interest, accompanying such conversations, and concerning which nothing appeared in the official correspondence. I kept such notes with particular consecutiveness during the years when I was director of the Chancellery of the Ministry for Foreign Affairs, which post included the duties attaching to the position of the Minister's Chef de Cabinet and Chief of the Political Section which embraced the whole of Western Europe and America. These notes were by no means intended for the Press. I also endeavoured to abstain from any expressions of my personal opinions in them, and in order still further to eliminate the personal element so far as I was concerned I always recorded the speeches included in them in the third person. The notes were intended to be unbiased and truthful chronicles of what I myself saw and heard. By this I do not wish to imply that I only wrote down that which I personally witnessed or in which I myself took part. On account of my duties as Chef de Cabinet, but still more so by reason of my long and close connection with my Chief, I was in a position to be constantly *au fait* of everything in which the Minister participated. The latter, on returning from an interview with the Tzar or after a discussion with any foreign ambassador or with his colleagues, the other Ministers, informed me while the impression was still fresh in his mind as to what he had said and done. Regarding this information imparted to me at first hand as being of special interest, it will be understood that I accorded it its due place in my notes, and with respect to this, if in reproducing the facts from S. D. Sazonov's words some small inexactitudes may here creep in at times as to details, I am certain that this was not the case with regard to the essentials.

Technically speaking, these notes were made as follows: Each day, whenever I succeeded in obtaining a free minute of spare time, I either rapidly wrote down a few lines in abbreviated form or dictated some short observations to one of the secretaries of the Chancellery, the talented Sleptzov, who, I regret, has come to his premature end, who then, either on the same day or at the latest on the following morning, copied them out on separate sheets of paper, which were simply added day by day to one another according to date in a special cupboard. During the two years July 1914 to July 1916, at which latter date I left the Ministry for Foreign Affairs, a large number of these separate sheets accumulated, and of these a small proportion has up to the present time been published in the *Red Archives*. It is true that the very fact of the preservation of these sheets in no way bound together might naturally lead to their being separated, and I am far from being sure that they have all been preserved in the archives of the Ministry as I put them together. On the contrary, I have some foundation for the supposition that amidst the disorder introduced by the Bolsheviki into all the Government establishments when they usurped power, and subsequently when the archives were transferred to Moscow, many pages of my diary might easily have been lost. This seems to be indicated by the fact, among other things, that as early as 1918 in the collection of documents belonging to the Ministry for Foreign Affairs issued by the Bolsheviki, there somehow chanced to appear a page of no particular interest, taken out of my diary. On the other hand, among the matter published in the *Red Archives* I fail to see certain notes referring to those same July days in 1914 of whose existence I have clear remembrance.

From my personal point of view I perhaps might regret now that I left the diary at the Ministry for Foreign Affairs, where it fell into the hands of the Bolsheviki, because if instead thereof it were now at my disposal, this would enable me on the foundation of those notes to follow the example of so many others and write my reminiscences. But, on the other hand, I welcome the manner in which things have turned out because the fact that the diary has been beyond my reach during all these years and has now been published in Moscow by my opponents without my desire or participation constitutes a great advantage, since it obviates all possibility of my being suspected of having compiled the notes *post factum* with some particular object in view. The diary is an original and unimpassioned relation of events written as these events occurred, without any ulterior object, and every unprejudiced reader will find in it fresh evidence of the sincere efforts made by the Imperial Russian Government to prevent war.

With regard to the form in which the diary has been published in the *Red Archives*, I deem it necessary to observe that the daily notes of an informatory character were my work. Simultaneously, and as far as I can recollect, there was also compiled every day in the Chancellery, on separate sheets of paper, an index of the more important telegrams and other official documents. Quite separate from all this was the report of the former Ambassador in Berlin, S. N. Sverbeev, written by him, so far as I know, on his journey from Germany to Russia via Sweden. The breaking up of this report into parts according to days and the insertion of it and of the official telegrams in my diary is the work of the hand of some later compiler or Bolshevist editor of the *Red Archives*. I do not consider it superfluous to call attention to this in view of the completely unfounded deductions drawn on the foundation of this edition of the " diary " by von Jagow, the former German Secretary of State for Foreign Affairs, who regards it as proof that the notes themselves were compiled at a period subsequent to the events to which they refer.

As a matter of fact, I should be glad if my notes, by serving as fresh evidence of the efforts of Russian diplomacy to avoid war, helped to dispose of the fable so insistently disseminated by the Germans to the effect that the war was caused by the Russian mobilization. In reality, at the time when the notes were written no such decisive influence was attributed to this matter as was attempted to ascribe to it subsequently. Meanwhile it is evident from the notes that Russia only gradually, and under the pressure of a sense of its indispensability, decided upon that measure, which, it goes without saying, could not justify the issuing of the German ultimatum, the more so because the Emperor Nicholas, in his telegram addressed to the Emperor Wilhelm, gave his word that, despite the mobilization, Russian troops should not undertake hostile action of any kind against Germany while negotiations directed towards a peaceful settlement of the crisis that had arisen continued.

Austria's attack upon Serbia impelled the Russian Government to carry out a partial mobilization of the four military districts for the purpose of exercising an effect upon Austria and restraining her from destroying Serbia. In connection therewith, it was hoped in St. Petersburg that Germany would for her part exert a moderating influence in Vienna, where not only was there no thought of mobilizing against Germany, but special endeavours were made to emphasize the fact that the mobilization of the four districts was in no way directed against her. Not until the return of the Emperor Wilhelm from his cruise to Norway did the ambiguity of German diplomacy begin to create disillusionment and raise doubts as to the possibility of maintaining peace. It became apparent that despite Germany's promise to exert a moderating influence on her ally, nothing of a serious nature was undertaken in this connection. It began, therefore, to be feared in Russia that we might be taken unawares by events and find ourselves face to face with a fully armed opponent before we had rendered our defence secure. It was only gradually that in Petersburg the belief developed that Germany could not be relied upon, and that her mediation could not be calculated on for the purpose of settling the Austro-Serbian conflict, which carried with it the danger of a European war,

Under the influence of these new conditions, General Yanushkevich, the Chief of the General Staff, saw S. D. Sazonov and explained to him that for technical reasons it would be impossible to pass from a partial to a general mobilization by simply promulgating an order to mobilize throughout the Empire. In General Yanushkevich's opinion, if the order to mobilize the four districts were carried out, and if subsequently fresh complications arose in our relations with Germany, Russia would be placed in a very unpleasant—indeed, perilous—position, because the plans for a general mobilization prepared in the Ministry for War could not be put into operation. General Yanushkevich, in view of this, requested Sazonov to give him a categorical assurance that war with Germany would be avoided. Sazonov replied that, to his regret, he was unable to give an undertaking of that kind, the more so because his own hopes of active assistance from Berlin in settling the conflict were steadily growing weaker. Under these circumstances it was, in General Yanushkevich's opinion, indispensable that Sazonov, who at that time enjoyed the special confidence of the Tzar, should draw His Majesty's attention to the dangers attending a partial mobilization. If I am not mistaken, this conversation of Sazonov's with General Yanushkevich took place at the Ministry for Foreign Affairs on the 28th of July. General Yanushkevich's arguments made a great impression on S. D. Sazonov. The Chief of the General Staff again insisted upon the indispensability of the measures proposed by him during his conversation with Sazonov on the following day, viz. the 29th of July. The Tzar, influenced by the arguments adduced, consented, although not at all willingly, to sign the order for a general mobilization, but under the impression produced by further and, as it seemed to him, more favourable telegrams from the Emperor Wilhelm, the Tzar that same evening cancelled the order for the general mobilization. Hopes and disappointments so rapidly succeeded one another during those alarming days, that a ray of hope which shone out on the evening of the 29th of July again vanished as early as the following morning. General Yanushkevich again saw Sazonov, and insisted upon the necessity for obtaining the Tzar's consent to a general mobilization. In the notes, S. D. Sazonov's report to the Tzar at Peterhof at the time when general mobilization was finally decided upon is written out in detail, and from these notes, composed at the time under the still fresh impressions of the moment, it will be seen with what difficulty this decision was come to only after every hope of preserving peace had vanished. The Russian mobilization therefore was not the cause of the war; the loss of all hope of averting war led Russia to mobilize her forces for the purpose of self-defence.

(*Signed*) M. SCHILLING.

LONDON,
  18*th April*, 1925.

PREFACE

AMONG the archives of the Chancellery of the Minister for Foreign Affairs there is preserved a diary of events during the period 3rd/20th of July, 1914 (old style). The documents published in due course in Russian official editions and in the official publications of other countries are placed on the left side of the page, with a reference to the place where they were published, while on the right side are written down the events occurring chiefly in St. Petersburg and telegrams and other documents connected with the crisis. This portion of the ministerial diary is printed in the following pages.

The diary was typewritten, and had manifestly not been submitted to final revision.

The diary only briefly records the contents of telegrams and in some cases merely indicates the numbers given to the telegrams. Consequently the full text of these telegrams is given in the appendixes. These telegrams are arranged, as is the case in the diary, in the consecutive order of their assigned numbers. Telegrams Nos. 1488, 1508, 1509, 1521, 1524, 1539, 1540, 1544, 1551, 1554, 1 and 2, 1555, 1582, 1583, 1592, 1601 and 1618 are not reproduced here, as they have already been published (see " Russo-German Relations," in the *Red Archives*, vol. i, pp. 167–188) and " Historical Data Regarding Franco-Russian Relations during the Period 1910–1914," edition published by the National Commissariat for Foreign Affairs, p. 520.

In connection with the telegrams of Nicholas II and Wilhelm II, the diary contains corrections regarding the times of their despatch and receipt. These corrections are reproduced here in footnotes. The note written by the former Russian Ambassador in Berlin, S. Sverbeev, in French, is broken up and arranged in the diary according to the dates to which the parts refer, and is similarly printed in the Russian translation. The original French text is reproduced in the appendix.

These materials were prepared for the Press by S. A. Pashookanis.

EDITOR.

CONTENTS

	PAGE
FOREWORD	5
INTRODUCTION	11
PREFACE	19
LIST OF NAMES OF PERSONAGES REFERRED TO IN THE DIARY	24
COMMENCEMENT OF THE DIARY, 3/16 JULY	25
DIARY, 4/17 JULY	26
DIARY, 5/18 JULY	26
9/22 JULY, TELEGRAM NO. 1475 TO VIENNA	27
DIARY, 10/23 JULY	28
DIARY, 11/24 JULY	28
Telegram No. 1487 to Belgrade	33
Telegram No. 1488 to Vienna, Paris, Berlin, London, Rome, Bukharest, Belgrade and Constantinople	33
Note, Count Pourtalès to S. D. Sazonov	33
DIARY, 12/25 JULY	34
Telegram No. 1489 to London	35
Telegram No. 1494 to Belgrade and London	35
Telegram No. 1496 to Constantinople, Sofia, Bukharest, Athens and Nisch	35
Aide Mémoire by British Ambassador	35
Telegram No. 1504 to Berlin, Vienna, Stockholm, Christiania, Copenhagen, Bukharest, Sofia and Constantinople	36
Telegram No. 1505 to Rome, London and Paris	37
Telegram No. 1508 to Vienna, London, Paris and Berlin	37
Telegram No. 1509 to Berlin	37
13/26 JULY, DISPATCH NO. 46 FROM THE CHARGÉ D'AFFAIRES IN VIENNA	37
DIARY, 14/27 JULY	41
Telegram No. 1514 to Berlin	42
Telegram No. 1521 to London, Paris, Berlin, Vienna and Rome	42
Telegram No. 1552 to Constantinople, Sofia and Bukharest	42
Telegram No. 1523 to Cettinje	42
Telegram No. 1524 to Paris, London, Vienna, Berlin, Rome and Constantinople	43
Telegram No. 1525 to Nisch	43
DIARY, 15/28 JULY	43
Telegram No. 1528 to London and Paris	43
Telegram No. 1529 to Paris and Constantinople	43
Telegram No. 1533 to Nisch	43
Telegram No. 1536 to Bukharest	44
Telegram No. 1537 to Constantinople	44
Telegram No. 1538 to London, Paris, Vienna, Berlin and Rome	44
Telegram No. 1539 to Berlin, Paris, London, Vienna and Rome	44
Telegram No. 1540 to Vienna, Paris, London and Rome	44
Telegram No. 1541 to Bukharest	45
Telegram No. 1 from Kaiser Wilhelm to the Emperor	45
Telegram No. 2 from the Emperor to Kaiser Wilhelm	46
DIARY, 16/29 JULY	47
Telegram No. 1541 to Bukharest	53
Telegram No. 1543 to Stockholm and Bukharest	53
Telegram No. 1544 to Berlin, Vienna, Rome, Nisch, London, Paris, Bukharest and Constantinople	53

		PAGE
Telegram No. 1547 to London, Paris and Nisch		53
Telegram No. 1548 to Paris, London, Vienna, Berlin, Rome, Constantinople, Bukharest and Nisch		54
Telegram No. 1551 to London and Paris		54
Telegram No. 1552 to Berlin and Sofia		54
Telegram No. 3 from the Tzar to Kaiser Wilhelm		54
Telegram No. 4 from Kaiser Wilhelm to the Tzar		55
Telegram No. 5 from the Tzar to Kaiser Wilhelm		56
Sverbeev's Note		56
DIARY, 17/30 JULY		62
Telegram No. 1554, Nos. 1 and 2 to Berlin		66
Telegram No. 1555 to Berlin, Paris, London and Vienna		66
Telegram No. 1556 to Bukharest		67
Telegram No. 1558 to London		67
Telegram No. 6 from Kaiser Wilhelm to the Tzar		67
Report by Sverbeev		68
DIARY, 18/31 JULY		69
Note by the German Ambassador		70
Telegram No. 1574 to Nisch		71
Telegram No. 1576 to Constantinople		71
Telegram No. 1579 to Bukharest		71
Telegram No. 1583 to Paris, London, Berlin, Vienna and Rome		71
Telegram No. 1582 to Paris, London, Berlin and Rome		72
Telegram No. 1587 to Nisch		72
Telegram No. 1589 to London and Paris		72
Telegram No. 1592 to Berlin, Vienna, Paris, London and Rome		72
Telegram No. 7 from the Tzar to Kaiser Wilhelm		72
Telegram No. 8 from Kaiser Wilhelm to the Tzar		73
Note by Sverbeev		74
DIARY, 19 JULY/1 AUGUST		76
Telegram No. 1601 to Paris, London, Berlin and Rome		79
Telegram No. 1603 to Stockholm		80
Telegram No. 1604 to San Sebastian		80
Telegram No. 1618 to the Imperial Representatives Abroad		80
Telegram No. 1622 to Vienna		80
Telegram No. 1624 to Vienna		81
Telegram No. 1627 to Paris and London		81
Telegram No. 9 from the Tzar to Kaiser Wilhelm		81
Note by Sverbeev		81
Telegram No. 10 from Kaiser Wilhelm to the Tzar		82
Letter from Count Pourtalès to the Minister for Foreign Affairs		83
Note by Sverbeev		83
APPENDIX I		85
Secret Telegram No. 1475 from the Foreign Minister to the Ambassador in Vienna		85
Secret Telegram No. 1487 to the Chargé d'Affaires, Belgrade		86
Secret Telegram No. 1489 from the Foreign Minister to the Ambassador in London		86
Secret Telegram No. 1494 from the Foreign Minister to the Chargé d'Affaires, Belgrade		87
Telegram to the Ambassador in London		88
Secret Telegram No. 1496 from the Foreign Minister to the Ambassador in Constantinople, the Ministers in Sofia and Bukharest and the Chargé d'Affaires at Athens		88
Aide Mémoire sent to Belgrade		89
Secret Telegram No. 1504 from the Foreign Minister to the Representatives in Vienna, Stockholm, Bukharest, Constantinople, Christiania and Copenhagen		90

CONTENTS

	PAGE
Secret Telegram No. 1505 from the Foreign Minister to the Ambassador at Rome	90
Secret Telegram No. 1506 from the Foreign Minister to the Minister at Bukharest	91
Secret Telegram No. 1514 from the Foreign Minister to the Chargé d'Affaires at Berlin	92
Secret Telegram No. 1522 from the Foreign Minister to the Representatives in Constantinople, Sofia and Bukharest	92
Secret Telegram No. 1523 from the Foreign Minister to the Minister at Cettinje	92
Secret Telegram No. 1525 to the Chargé d'Affaires at Belgrade	93
Secret Telegram No. 1528 from the Foreign Minister to the Ambassador in London	94
Secret Telegram No. 1536 to the Minister at Bukharest	94
Secret Telegram No. 1537 to the Ambassador at Constantinople	95
Secret Telegram No. 1538 from the Foreign Minister to the Ambassador in London	95
Secret Telegram No. 1541 from the Foreign Minister to the Minister at Bukharest	96
Secret Telegram No. 1543 to the Ministers in Stockholm and Bukharest	96
Secret Telegram No. 1547 from the Foreign Minister to the Ambassadors in Paris and London and the Chargé d'Affaires in Serbia	97
Secret Telegram No. 1548 from the Foreign Minister to the Ambassadors in Paris and London	97
Secret Telegram No. 1556 from the Foreign Minister to the Minister at Bukharest	98
Secret Telegram No. 1558 from the Foreign Minister to the Ambassador in London	98
Secret Telegram No. 1576 from the Foreign Minister to the Chargé d'Affaires in Serbia	98
Secret Telegram No. 1579 to the Minister at Bukharest	99
Secret Telegram No. 1587 from the Foreign Minister to the Chargé d'Affaires at Nisch	100
Secret Telegram No. 1589 from the Foreign Minister to the Ambassador in London	100
Secret Telegram No. 1603 from the Foreign Minister to the Minister at Stockholm	100
Secret Telegram No. 1604 from the Foreign Minister to the Ambassador in Madrid	101
Secret Telegram No. 1622 from the Foreign Minister to the Ambassador in Vienna	101
Secret Telegram No. 1624 from the Foreign Minister to the Ambassador in Vienna	101
Secret Telegram No. 1627 from the Foreign Minister to the Ambassador in London	102
Sverbeev's Note (Original Text)	102
APPENDIX II	113
The Tzar's Speech to M. Poincaré	113
M. Poincaré's Reply	114
M. Poincaré's Speech to the Tzar	115
The Tzar's Reply	115
Extract from Sukhomlinov's "Recollections"	116
Secret Telegram No. 140 from the Ambassador in Berlin	118
Secret Telegram No. 146 from the Ambassador in Berlin	120
Secret Telegram No. 147 from the Ambassador in Berlin	121

LIST OF NAMES OF PERSONAGES REFERRED TO IN THE DIARY OF THE FORMER RUSSIAN MINISTRY FOR FOREIGN AFFAIRS

BELDIMAN: Rumanian Minister in Berlin in 1914.

BRATIANU: Rumanian Premier and Minister for War in 1914.

GIESL, BARON: Austrian Minister in 1914.

KLEINMICHEL, MARIA EDUARDOVNA, née COUNTESS KELLER, who held a Germanophile salon in Petersburg.

MONKEVITZ, NIKOLAI AUGUSTOVICH: Assistant to the first Chief Quartermaster of the Head Administration of the General Staff in 1914.

NERATOV, ANATOL ANATOLIEVICH: Assistant to the Minister for Foreign Affairs in 1914.

PASHICH: Serbian Prime Minister and Foreign Minister in 1914.

TATISTCHEV, ILYA LEONIDOVICH: Major-General à la suite. Attached to the German Kaiser since December 1905.

FACHREDDIN: Turkish Ambassador in Petersburg in 1914.

ZIMMERMANN: German Under-Secretary of State in the Ministry for Foreign Affairs in 1914.

SHEBEKO, NIKOLAI NIKOLAIEVICH: Russian Ambassador in Vienna in 1914.

SCHILLING, MORITZ FABIANOVICH, BARON: Chief of the Chancellery of the Minister for Foreign Affairs in 1914.

HOW THE WAR BEGAN IN 1914

3/16 July.

At an evening party at Countess Kleinmichel's the Italian Ambassador asked Baron Schilling what attitude Russia would adopt should Austria decide to take action of any kind against Serbia. Baron Schilling replied without hesitation that Russia would not endure any infringement by Austria of the integrity and independence of Serbia. The Marquis Carlotti remarked that if this was Russia's firm determination it would be well that she should make a plain representation to Vienna to that effect, because it was his impression that Austria was capable of taking an irrevocable step with regard to Serbia, based on the belief that although Russia would make a verbal protest, she would not adopt forcible measures for the protection of Serbia against any Austrian attempts. If, however, Vienna had to reckon with the unavoidability of a collision with Russia, in all probability the Government there would begin to consider the results of adopting a too energetic policy with regard to Serbia.

Baron Schilling said to the Ambassador that he was in a position to emphasize his declaration that Russia was firmly determined not to permit any weakening or humiliation of Serbia, and it was therefore the duty of Austria's allies to warn her of the dangers arising from her present policy, as Russia's determination to protect the independence of Serbia could no longer be doubted.

The Ambassador promised to telegraph to Rome to this effect and to request the Italian Government to draw the attention of the Vienna Cabinet to the foregoing, but remarked that in his opinion it would produce a greater impression in Vienna if a declaration of this sort were made there by Russia herself rather than by Italy, which was an ally.[1]

Baron Schilling said to the Ambassador that, on the contrary, if Russia made such a declaration in Vienna it would perhaps be regarded as an ultimatum, and so render the situation more acute, whereas insistent advice proffered by Italy and Germany—that is, by allies—would certainly be more acceptable to Austria-Hungary.

4/17 July

Return from leave of the Austro-Hungarian Ambassador.

Count Szapary, the Austro-Hungarian Ambassador, on returning from leave, expressed a desire to see the Minister as soon as possible. He was told in reply that S. D. Sazonov, who had gone into the country for a few days, was expected back in Petersburg to-morrow morning, and would be ready to receive the Ambassador at 11 a.m. on that day.

5/18 July.

S. D. Sazonov returned from a short country excursion. Wishing to render himself *au fait* as

[1] Up to the present no telegram from the Italian Ambassador on this subject has become known. It therefore remains an open question whether the Italian Ambassador telegraphed to Rome in this sense.

to the state of affairs prior to his meeting with the Austrian Ambassador, Baron Schilling went to meet him at the terminus, and on the way from thence to the Ministry acquainted him with the contents of a telegram (No. 88) [1] received from N. N. Shebeko in Vienna on the preceding evening, and also with his conversation with the Italian Ambassador on July 3rd. The Minister was troubled by this information, and agreed with Baron Schilling as to the necessity for forewarning Austria regarding the determination of Russia on no account to permit any attempts against the independence of Serbia. The Minister formed the resolve to express himself in the most decided manner to the Austro-Hungarian Ambassador regarding this matter.

Soon after reaching the Ministry, S. D. Sazonov received Count Szapary, who spoke in the most peaceable manner of an entire absence in Austria of any intention of rendering relations with Serbia more acute. His assurances were so positive that they completely quieted the Minister's apprehensions, so much so that after this interview he said to Baron Schilling that he had had no need to resort to threats, as the Austro-Hungarian Ambassador had sufficiently emphatically assured him of the love of peace of his Government. " Il a été doux comme un agneau."

PETERSBURG. 9/22 JULY.

TELEGRAM TO VIENNA, DISPATCHED 4 A.M. NO. 1475.

Please be so good as to point out in a friendly but firm manner the dangerous consequences of any action

[1] Shebeko's telegram No. 88 here referred to is not included in the Russian Orange Book and has not hitherto been published anywhere else.

on the part of Austria of an unacceptable character with regard to the dignity of Serbia. The French and English Ambassadors in Vienna have been instructed to suggest a policy of moderation.

SAZONOV.

10/23 JULY.

After dinner, at 9 p.m., Count Montereale, Councillor of the Italian Embassy, said to K. E. Butzov, who is in charge of the Near East Section of the Foreign Office in the absence of Prince Troubetzkoi, that according to information just received by the Italian Embassy Austria-Hungary would to-day present to Serbia a quite unacceptable ultimatum. Up to a late hour of the night nothing was known of this either at the Ministry for Foreign Affairs, the French and English Embassies, or at the telegraph agency. During the evening Count Szapary, the Austrian Ambassador, requested by telephone that the Minister would name an hour at which to see him on the following day.

11/24 JULY.

Early this morning a telegram was received at the Foreign Office from Belgrade confirming the information given yesterday by the Councillor of the Italian Embassy. Baron Schilling immediately warned the Ambassadors Isvolsky and Shebeko of the necessity of their returning immediately to their posts.[1]

Towards 10 a.m. S. D. Sazonov arrived from Tzarskoe Selo, when Baron Schilling immediately communicated the above-mentioned information to him, which created a very strong impression upon the Minister, who at once exclaimed: "C'est la guerre

---

[1] Not published hitherto.

européenne." The Austro-Hungarian Ambassador was at once called to the Ministry by telephone, and while awaiting him S. D. Sazonov reported to the Tzar by telephone from Baron Schilling's office regarding Austria's ultimatum to Serbia. His Majesty exclaimed, "This is disturbing," and gave orders to keep him informed as to the further course of events.

Meanwhile the Austro-Hungarian Ambassador arrived and handed to the Minister a copy of the Austrian note to Serbia. At the same time Baron Schilling, in the name of the Minister, informed the Ministers for War, Marine and Finance of the course of affairs and, on the instruction of S. D. Sazonov, warned them to attend the sitting of the Council of Ministers without fail. At the request of Admiral Grigorovich, Baron Schilling sent a similar communication to Admiral Rusin, the Chief of the Naval General Staff. The Minister of Finance had only just returned from reporting to the Tzar, from whom he had already learned of the step taken by Austria in Belgrade. Baron Schilling pointed out to P. L. Bark the necessity in any case of at once withdrawing as far as possible all our State deposits in Germany.

A. A. Neratov, Prince Troubetzkoi, and all the officials of the Ministers' Chancellery and of the Near East Section, were at once recalled from leave by telegraph.

The French Ambassador after breakfast called together for an exchange of opinions S. D. Sazonov, and the English Ambassador and the Rumanian Minister.[1] The Minister pressed these representatives to communicate to their respective Governments his

[1] Compare Buchanan's report to Grey of the 24th of July (English Blue Book No. 6), in which the summoning of the Rumanian Minister to the discussion concerning the common plan of action is not mentioned.

request that they would immediately elaborate with us a plan of action. This request was naturally addressed to the Rumanian Minister as well, so that Rumania was thereby drawn into this matter of general concern. It was of the greatest advantage for us that Rumania should be drawn in on our side, while for Rumania it was manifestly flattering to participate as an equal in the diplomatic steps taken by the Great Powers.

The Council of Ministers met at 3 p.m., at which S. D. Sazonov reported regarding the course of the negotiations arising from the handing of the threatening note to Serbia on the previous day by Austria-Hungary. The Council of Ministers expressed approval of the proposals of the Foreign Minister, viz. (1) In conjunction with the other Powers to request Austria to prolong the period which she had fixed for the receipt of a reply from Serbia in order to afford the Powers time in which to acquaint themselves, in accordance with the proposal of Austria herself, with the results of the judicial inquiry into the Serajevo assassination; and (2) to advise Serbia not to enter into hostilities with Austro-Hungarian troops, but, withdrawing her own forces, to request the Powers to compose the quarrel that had arisen. At the same time it was decided in principle to mobilize four military districts (Odessa, Kiev, Moscow, Kazan) and the two fleets (Baltic and Black Sea) and to take other military measures should circumstances so require. In this connection attention was turned to the fact that all military preparations were clearly and exclusively directed with a view to the possibility of a conflict with Austria-Hungary, and could not be represented as unfriendly actions with regard to Germany.

After the Council meeting there was an interview between S. D. Sazonov and the Serbian Minister, during which the former advised extreme moderation in respect of the Serbian reply to the Austrian note.

At 7 p.m. the German Ambassador came to the Foreign Office. He endeavoured to justify Austria's action on the grounds that the investigation with regard to the Serajevo assassination established the guilt of the Serbian Government. In addition, he endeavoured to establish the correctness of the Austrian procedure by reason of the necessity for protecting the " monarchical principle." S. D. Sazonov addressed Count Pourtalès in a very firm manner, and sharply criticized the Vienna Cabinet, insisting upon the unacceptable nature of the note to Serbia and the lack of courtesy towards the Great Powers in that Austria, in turning to them at the same time accorded to Serbia so short a period wherein to meet her demands that the Powers were not afforded a possibility of considering the matter and giving their observations in time to be of avail.

Those who saw Count Pourtalès as he left the Ministry state that he was very agitated, and did not conceal the fact that S. D. Sazonov's words, and especially his firm determination to resist the Austrian demands, had made a strong impression upon him.

While the German Ambassador was with the Minister the French Ambassador arrived at the Foreign Office and, not wishing to meet his German colleague, went to Baron Schilling and waited with him in his cabinet until the Minister was free, as Count Pourtalès could not pass through here. The French Ambassador meanwhile expressed the opinion that despite the events which had occurred he considered that the

President of the French Republic ought not to change in any respect the programme for his journey to the Scandinavian capitals, but should return quietly to France, as previously proposed, after making halts at Stockholm and Copenhagen. Otherwise, in the opinion of the Ambassador a general panic might arise, because there would be an impression that the head of the French Republic regarded the political situation as threatening. Meanwhile the Ambassador considered the situation as by no means hopeless. He founded his optimism upon the supposition that Germany would scarcely decide to support Austria since she knew to what serious consequences this would inevitably lead at the present moment. " Jamais nous n'avons été en meilleure posture," he said, " car nous sommes parfaitement d'accord entre nous et ce n'est point là une appreciation d'Ambassadeur, mais nous avons 4 documents récents de tres grande importance qui l'attestent." Baron Schilling, somewhat astonished, asked the Ambassador what was the nature of these four, apparently to him, unknown documents which were of such great importance that in presence of them Germany would have to call a halt even if she desired to go to war for the purpose of supporting her ally Austria. It appeared that M. Paléologue regarded as such documents the speeches recently exchanged by the Emperor and the President of the French Republic at Peterhof and on board the battleship *France*.

Immediately after the departure of Count Pourtalès the French Ambassador was received by the Minister, who promptly informed him of the decisions come to by the Council of Ministers, and also concerning his conversations with the Serbian Minister and the German Ambassador.

TELEGRAM TO BELGRADE. NO. 1487.

In view of the helpless situation of the Serbians, it would be better for them to offer no resistance, but to address an appeal to the Great Powers.

SAZONOV.

TELEGRAM TO VIENNA, PARIS, BERLIN, LONDON, ROME, BUKHAREST, BELGRADE AND CONSTANTINOPLE. NO. 1488.

Austria-Hungary informed the Powers of her step only twelve hours after presenting her ultimatum to Belgrade. We consider it indispensable that she should prolong the period accorded to Serbia in which to reply. If Austria enables the Powers to acquaint themselves with the results of the investigation, they would be in a position to give Serbia corresponding advice.

The German, French, English, Italian and Rumanian Governments are being asked to support our action.

SAZONOV.

A copy of the Austro-Hungarian note to Serbia was handed to S. D. Sazonov by Count Szapary at 11 a.m.[1]

NOTE HANDED TO S. D. SAZONOV BY COUNT POURTALÈS.

We learn from an authoritative source that the news disseminated by some journals to the effect that the démarche of the Austro-Hungarian Govern-

---

[1] The text of the Austrian ultimatum is so widely known that it is omitted from the appendix to this volume.—*Editor's note.*

ment in Belgrade was made at the instigation of the German Government is absolutely false. The German Government had no knowledge of the text of the Austrian note prior to its dispatch, and has exercised no influence whatever upon its contents. It is therefore wrong to attribute a threatening attitude to Germany.

As the ally of Austria, Germany naturally supports the demands presented by the Vienna Cabinet to Serbia, which are, in her opinion, justified.

She desires above all, as she already declared before the commencement of the Austro-Serbian conflict, that it should remain localized.

12/25 JULY.

The Minister who arrived from Tzarskoe Selo at 9 a.m. came to the Foreign Office only for a few minutes in order to inform himself with regard to telegrams received during the night, and then immediately returned to Tzarskoe Selo, where, under the presidency of H.M. the Emperor, a Council of the Ministers concerned with the defence of the Empire was called together. At this conference the decisions arrived at on the preceding evening by the Council of Ministers were approved and further developed. It was decided not to order mobilization as yet, but to undertake all the preparatory measures for accelerating it should it become a necessity.

During the day information was received from London and Paris to the effect that the Austro-Hungarian diplomats there emphasize the difference between an ultimatum and a simple note à terme such as, in their words, the note handed in at Belgrade by the Austrian Minister on the 10th of July constitutes. Taking their stand upon this, the said diplomats endeavour to show that even in the event of an unsatisfactory reply by Serbia, military action need not immediately follow. By reason of those reports there is apparent to-day among the foreign diplomats in Petersburg, especially on the part of the French Ambassador and the Rumanian Minister, a more optimistic estimate of events and hope of a favourable solution of the crisis.

TELEGRAM No 1489 SENT TO LONDON.

The attitude which England adopts is of prime importance. England could exercise a moderating influence on Austria. Should the situation become more acute, we rely upon England to stand for the defence of the European balance.   SAZONOV.

TELEGRAM No. 1494 TO BELGRADE AND LONDON.

In view of England's attitude, war between Serbia and Austria can perhaps be prevented if Serbia approaches England with a request for mediation.

SAZONOV.

TELEGRAM No. 1496 SENT TO CONSTANTINOPLE, SOFIA, BUKHAREST, ATHENS AND NISCH. (To Nisch under No. 1576.)

Negotiations are proceeding between Turkey, Bulgaria and Austria.

AIDE MÉMOIRE HANDED IN BY THE AMBASSADOR OF GREAT BRITAIN ON THE 12/25 JULY, 1914.[1]

The Austro-Hungarian Ambassador in London has been authorized to explain to Sir E. Grey that the

[1] This aide mémoire is missing in the original text of the Foreign Office diary. See appendix.—*Editor's note.*

step taken at Belgrade was not an "ultimatum," but a "démarche" with a time limit, and that if the Austrian demands were not complied with within that limit the Austro-Hungarian Government would break off diplomatic relations with Serbia and begin military preparations, not operations.

His Majesty's Ambassador is instructed by Sir Edward Grey to communicate the above information to the Imperial Minister for Foreign Affairs as soon as possible in case the Austro-Hungarian Government has not made the same explanation at St. Petersburg, as the immediate situation is thereby rendered less acute.

On the aide mémoire His Majesty wrote, "playing with words." Peterhof, July 13, 1914.

AIDE MÉMOIRE HANDED IN BY THE AMBASSADOR OF GREAT BRITAIN ON THE 12/25 JULY, 1914.

Copy attached.

(NOTE.—This aide mémoire is wanting in the original text of the Foreign Office diary. See appendix.)[1]

TELEGRAM No 1504 TO BERLIN, VIENNA, STOCKHOLM, CHRISTIANIA, COPENHAGEN, BUKHAREST, SOFIA AND CONSTANTINOPLE.

Communicate regarding the military measures adopted in countries adjoining us.

SAZONOV.

[1] Neither the aide mémoire nor a copy of it appears in the appendix.—W. C. B., *translator*.

TELEGRAM No. 1505 TO ROME, LONDON AND PARIS.

We are of opinion that Italy could play a part of the first importance by bringing her influence to bear on Austria.

SAZONOV.

TELEGRAM No. 1508 TO VIENNA, LONDON, PARIS AND BERLIN.

Having examined together with the Austro-Hungarian Ambassador the ten demands presented to Serbia, I pointed out that besides their infelicitous form some of them were in substance incapable of fulfilment. With regard to the others, it was possible to find a basis for agreement. It was desirable that the Austro-Hungarian Ambassador should be empowered to enter into a partial exchange of ideas with me for the purpose of amending some of the paragraphs of the note.

SAZONOV.

TELEGRAM No. 1509 TO BERLIN.

Request the German Government to advise Vienna to accept our proposals.

SAZONOV.

DISPATCH FROM THE CHARGÉ D'AFFAIRES IN VIENNA 13/26 JULY, 1914. No. 46.[1]

I have the honour to present to your Excellency the following exposition of events which have occurred in Vienna between the 10th and 12th of July in so far

---

[1] Not published hitherto.

as the Embassy entrusted to my charge has participated in them. Even as late as Thursday morning nothing pointed to that dramatic change in the situation occasioned by the handing in of the Austrian ultimatum to the Serbian Government that same evening. Rumours concerning the step to be taken by Austria in Belgrade continued just as during the preceding three weeks in society and in the Press, but by no means in the sense of any gradual growth of a feeling of anger against Serbia. As before, official circles of various shades of opinion indulged in polemics against the Serbian journals, and, also as before, the opposition papers mocked at the attempts of the Government to exert pressure upon Serbia in a sense favourable to Austria-Hungary, and as early as Wednesday evening I happened to hear a report emanating from the Court at Ischl to the effect that the demands to be presented to Belgrade were not drawn up in a hostile spirit. At about 3 p.m. on Thursday, July 10th, I received your Excellency's telegram No. 1475 of the 9th. Without awaiting an interview with the French and English Ambassadors, I immediately asked Count Berchtold when he could see me. The reply was that the Minister was busy to-day (as a matter of fact, he took part in the sitting of the Council of Ministers), but invited me to come to him at 11 a.m. on the morrow. I utilized this delay to discuss the situation with M. Dumaine and Sir M. Bunsen that same evening. It appeared that both these Ambassadors had visited the Ballplatz together at about 5 p.m., and had academic conversations with the chiefs of sections—M. Dumaine with Baron Macchio and Sir M. Bunsen with Count Forgach. The replies of these two Austrian diplomats to the inquiries of the Ambassadors as to when Austria-

Hungary proposed to take action at Belgrade were characteristic. Baron Macchio replied evasively that this would be soon—probably next day. Meanwhile at that very time when these words were uttered Baron Giesl was presenting the ultimatum to Belgrade. Count Forgach did not conceal this fact from the English Ambassador, but also added that the note (he did not term it an ultimatum) was drawn up in a sharp tone, "as it is no use speaking to Serbia in any other way," and that in any case it was in essence entirely acceptable and capable of fulfilment.

This information I immediately brought to your notice by telegram No. 89.

The next morning all the newspapers published the full text of the ultimatum. Thereby the original object of my visit to the Foreign Minister when I presented myself to him on the following morning at 11 o'clock was anticipated. I reproduced the substance of my interview with Count Berchtold in my telegrams to you, Nos. 90 and 91 of the 11/24 July. The essence of it was contained in the declaration of the Minister as to what constituted the underlying motive of Austria's outburst. "All are firmly convinced," he said, "and in the first place the Emperor himself (and who can doubt his love of peace, especially when his age is considered?) that the purpose of the all-Serbian propaganda is to undermine our house, our dynasty. To endure it any longer would be to confess the downfall of the monarchy. The destruction of this propaganda, root and branch, is a matter of life or death for Austria-Hungary as a Great Power. We must show that we are a Great Power. The existence of Austria-Hungary is necessary to the European balance of power, and I am persuaded that the Imperialists in Russia think so too. They cannot desire the ruin of Austria-Hungary if only in the interests of the maintenance of the monarchical principle." Such words, in the mouth of Count Berchtold, who is by no means generally inclined to the utterance of observations of a politico-philosophical nature, reflect deep conviction, if not on his own part, then at any rate on the part of those responsible for the decision taken by Austria. These convictions lead to the final conclusion that Serbia, with her nationalist, extremely democratic, purely "lay" (in the sense of opposition to clericalism) propaganda, undoubtedly represents a real threat to the Austro-Hungarian State, which is founded upon Roman Catholic clericalism and the relics of a defunct feudalism. From this it follows that it is clearly indispensable to Austria-Hungary to cut through the roots of this ever-growing threatening danger before it is too late, and to profit by the most favourable opportunity, such as the present is recognized to be, for doing so. Only in this way can be explained the undoubted determination of the Government to proceed to a finish with the execution of Serbia. In this sense the rejection by the Imperial Government on Saturday, July 12th, of the endeavour made in Vienna through me to obtain a prolongation of the period in which a reply must be received, as contemplated by the Austrian ultimatum, is comprehensible. I will not again enter into the details regarding the carrying out of your instructions concerning this matter, as they are contained in my telegrams Nos. 95 and 96 of July 12th, and now possess only a passing interest.

Accept, etc., etc.

(*Signed*) KUDASCHEV.

14/27 JULY.

The Rumanian Minister informed Baron Schilling that in reply to his telegram to Bukharest sent at the request of S. D. Sazonov, pointing out the desirability of Rumania associating herself with the representation made to Vienna by the Great Powers regarding the prolongation of the period of delay accorded to Serbia, Bratianu had replied that owing to the limited time available he regretted he could not accede to this request. At the same time Bratianu informed M. Diamandi regarding an announcement made to him by the Austro-Hungarian Minister at Bukharest to the effect that Austria-Hungary was not seeking after any increase of territory at the expense of Serbia and that if it became necessary for her to enter into military occupation of any part of Serbia this would only be a temporary measure. Baron Schilling retorted that such a pronouncement was of but little value coming from Austria, who, as the example of Bosnia and Herzegovina showed to all the world, made clear what she understood by the term "temporary occupation of a foreign country." Here Baron Schilling reminded M. Diamandi of the latter's own words addressed to himself, Baron Schilling, at the time when they were travelling through Hungarian territory near Predeal six weeks ago, viz. that the interests of Serbia and Rumania were completely identical, and compel Rumania to stand firmly at the side of Serbia in the event of any attempts upon the latter on the part of Austria. The Rumanian Minister did not attempt to deny having spoken thus, but, on the contrary, declared that he continued to hold this opinion and was therefore all the more desirous that the present Austro-Serbian dispute should not lead to war, since this would place Rumania in a particularly difficult position.

Telegram No. 1514 to Berlin.

(This telegram is missing from the original text.)[1]

Telegram No. 1521 to London, Paris, Berlin, Vienna and Rome.

The English Ambassador asked our opinion as to the advisability of calling together a conference of the four Great Powers in London. I replied that if our direct representations to the Vienna Cabinet were unavailing I was prepared to accept the English proposal.

We are of opinion that the exercise of a moderating influence in Petersburg will become impossible if we oppose the acceptable demands made by Austria.

SAZONOV.

Telegram No. 1552 to Constantinople, Sofia and Bukharest.

Instructions for the reporting to the commander of the Black Sea forces of all movements of Turkish, Bulgarian and Rumanian warships.

SAZONOV.

Telegram No. 1523 to Cetinje.

Montenegro should observe a waiting and pacificatory attitude, and conform her policy to that of Serbia.

SAZONOV.

---

[1] This telegram is missing from the original text. See appendix.—*Editor's note.*

TELEGRAM No. 1524 TO PARIS, LONDON, VIENNA, BERLIN, ROME AND CONSTANTINOPLE.

By its moderation the Serbian reply transcends all our expectations.

SAZONOV.

TELEGRAM No. 1525 TO NISCH.

Reply telegram of H.M. the Emperor to King Alexander.

15/28 JULY.

On the instructions of his Government the French Ambassador acquainted the Foreign Minister with the complete readiness of France to fulfil her obligations as an ally in case of necessity.

TELEGRAM No. 1528 TO LONDON AND PARIS.

From a conversation with the German Ambassador the impression arises that Germany favours the unappeasable attitude of Austria. English influence in Berlin is desirable.

TELEGRAM No. 1529 TO PARIS AND CONSTANTINOPLE.

Confirmation of the news regarding the purchase of Turkey of the super-dreadnought *Admiral Togo*.

NERATOV.

TELEGRAM No. 1533 TO NISCH.

Prince Troubetzkoi has been appointed Minister to Serbia.

TELEGRAM No. 1536 TO BUKHAREST.

Personal.

TELEGRAM No. 1537 TO CONSTANTINOPLE.

You may announce that we are adopting general measures of precaution.

SAZONOV.

TELEGRAM No. 1538 TO LONDON, PARIS, VIENNA, BERLIN AND ROME.

In consequence of the declaration by Austria of war against Serbia, my mediatory explanations are rendered purposeless. The immediate mediation of England is indispensable, and also the stoppage of military action on the part of Austria, which might meanwhile crush Serbia.

SAZONOV.

TELEGRAM No. 1539 TO BERLIN, PARIS, LONDON, VIENNA AND ROME.

In consequence of Austria's declaration of war we shall announce to-morrow the mobilization of four military districts. Emphasize to the German Government the absence on the part of Russia of any aggressive intentions regarding Germany.

SAZONOV.

TELEGRAM No. 1540 TO VIENNA, PARIS, LONDON AND ROME.

Instructions to announce the declaration of mobilization.

TELEGRAM NO. 1541 TO BUKHAREST.
Possibility of Rumania's participation in the war.

SAZONOV.

TELEGRAM[1] NO. 1 OF KAISER WILHELM TO THE EMPEROR.

It is with the gravest concern that I hear of the impression which the action of Austria against Servia is creating in your country. The unscrupulous agitation that has been going on in Servia for years has resulted in the outrageous crime to which Archduke Franz Ferdinand fell a victim. The spirit that led Servians to murder their own King and his wife still dominates the country. You will doubtless agree with me that we both, you and me, have a common interest, as well as all Sovereigns, to insist that all the persons morally responsible for the dastardly murder should receive their deserved punishment. In this case politics play no part at all.

On the other hand, I fully understand how difficult it is for you and your Government to face the drift of your public opinion. Therefore, with regard to the hearty and tender friendship which binds us both from long ago with firm ties, I am exerting my utmost influence to induce the Austrians to deal straightly to arrive at a satisfactory understanding with you. I confidently hope you will help me in my efforts to smooth over difficulties that may still arise.

Your very sincere and devoted friend and cousin.

[1] Compare *German Documents* No. 335, according to which this telegram was dispatched at 1.45 a.m.

This telegram and all the subsequent communications between the two Emperors are reproduced here without correction of the English, in which the originals were written.—W. C. B., *translator.*

Above this telegram there is the following note in ink: "In order to fix exactly the times of dispatch and receipt of His Majesty's telegrams of the 28th of October, 1915, a question was addressed to the head of the Post and Telegraph Department. According to the information received from this source, Kaiser Wilhelm's telegram No. 113 from Friedrichshafen was given out on the 13/26 July at 3.15 p.m., and delivered to the Tzar at 8.10 a.m. on the 14th."

In the heading of the telegram there is inserted in pencil after the word "Berlin" the words, "10.45 p.m. according to the White Book." The number is omitted. (According to the German White Book, the telegram was dispatched on the 28th of July at 10.45 p.m. See *Das Deutsche Weissbuch*, p. 42.)

After the text of the telegram there is written in pencil: "Was not this telegram received by His Majesty on the 16th of July? The reply to it was sent on the 16th, during the day. There is proof of the receipt by His Majesty of Kaiser Wilhelm's telegram during the day of the 16th, as he telephoned to S. D. Sazonov concerning it."—*Editor's note*.

TELEGRAM NO. 2 FROM H.M. THE EMPEROR TO KAISER WILHELM.[1]

Am glad you are back. In this most serious moment I appeal to you to help me. An ignoble war has been declared on a weak country. The indignation in Russia, shared fully by me, is enormous. I foresee that very soon I shall be overwhelmed by the pressure brought upon me and forced to take extreme measures which will lead to war. To try to avoid such a calamity as a European war I beg you in the name of

[1] On the copy of this telegram written by N. Romanov himself, which is preserved in No. II department of the Archives Office, the date, "15 July, 1914," is written by his own hand. In the diary, after the heading of the telegram there is written in pencil, "1 p.m., according to the White Book, 29th July." After the text of the telegram there is written in ink, "Given out at Peterhof 00.29 a.m. No. 140."

HOW THE WAR BEGAN IN 1914

our old friendship to do what you can to stop your allies from going too far.

16/29 JULY.

At 9.30 this morning the German Ambassador called up Baron Schilling on the telephone and said that he desired to see the Minister in order to make to him an "agreeable communication." Count Pourtalès, however, hastened to add, "Toutefois pas trop d'optimisme." Baron Schilling replied that latterly we had grown unaccustomed to "pleasant" news from Berlin, and that therefore the Minister would certainly hear with pleasure what the Ambassador had to say.

S. D. Sazonov received Count Pourtalès at 11 a.m., who said that Germany was agreeable to continuing the attempts she had already made to induce the Vienna Cabinet to grant concessions. He requested, however, that strict secrecy should be maintained concerning this, as the announcement of such an intention on the part of the German Government might create the impression that the views of Austria and Germany were not fully in agreement in the present instance. In addition, the Ambassador insistently requested that the successful issue of the influence which Germany hoped to exercise in Vienna might not be hindered by a premature mobilization on our part.

After the Ambassador's departure the above-mentioned communication made by him was discussed by the Minister with A. A. Neratov, Baron Schilling and Prince Troubetzkoi. The question was raised whether Germany really intended to exert serious pressure in Vienna or whether the communication which Count Pourtalès was instructed to make was only intended to lull us to sleep and so to postpone the Russian mobilization and thus gain time wherein to make corresponding preparations. The general impression was that even if the sincerity of the German Government could be admitted, under the circumstances the possibility of arriving at any practical results in this direction must be doubted, because if Austria had gone thus far without the co-operation, or at least the tacit approval, of Germany, then it must be supposed that the influence of the latter in Vienna had greatly declined, and that therefore the German Government would not succeed in effecting much there at present.

At 3 p.m. the German Ambassador came again to the Minister and read to him a telegram from the Imperial Chancellor, in which it was stated that if Russia continued her military preparations, even though she did not proceed to mobilize, Germany would find herself compelled to mobilize, in which case she would immediately proceed to take the offensive. To this communication S. D. Sazonov sharply replied, " Maintenant je n'ai plus de doute sur les vraies causes de l'intransigeance autrichienne." [1]

Count Pourtalès jumped up from his seat, and also sharply exclaimed, " Je proteste de toutes mes forces, M. le Ministre, contre cette assertion blessante."

[1] This is telegram No. 134, and No. 342 of the *German Documents*. The telegram was handed in at the chief telegraph office at 12.50 p.m., and, according to the records of the Embassy in Petersburg, reached Petersburg at 4.35 p.m. It is therefore impossible that this telegram could have been read by the German Ambassador during a conversation with Sazonov at 3 p.m. The assertion that this conversation took place at 3 p.m., moreover, does not agree with that of Count Pourtalès, according to whom it took place between 6 and 7 p.m. Compare Pourtalès, *am Scheidewege*, p. 45, and No. 378 of the *German Documents*.

HOW THE WAR BEGAN IN 1914

The Minister drily replied that Germany still had an opportunity for proving the erroneousness of what he had said. The Minister and the Ambassador parted coolly.

Soon after the German Ambassador's departure, while A. A. Neratov and Baron Schilling were still in the Minister's cabinet, the telephone bell rang, and H.M. the Emperor personally informed S. D. Sazonov that he had just received a telegram from Kaiser Wilhelm, who urgently requested him not to allow events to develop into a war. S. D. Sazonov utilized this opportunity to report to His Majesty concerning the announcement made to him a few minutes previously by Count Pourtalès, and pointed out how little the words of the Kaiser agreed with the instructions conveyed to his Ambassador. The Tzar said that he was instantly telegraphing to Berlin to ask for an explanation of this apparent contradiction. His Majesty gave permission to S. D. Sazonov to discuss the question of our mobilization at once with the Minister for War and the Chief of the General Staff.

At this moment news was received of the commencement of the bombardment of Belgrade by the Austrians.

The discussion between the three above-mentioned persons took place soon afterwards in the cabinet of Lieut.-General Yanushkevich. In the adjoining room were Quartermaster-General Danilov, General Monkevitz, and the Assistant to the Chief of the Chancellery of the Foreign Minister, N. A. Basili, in readiness to immediately carry out the arrangements necessitated by the decisions about to be come to. Those decisions were awaited with some trepidation, since all concerned knew how important in respect of our military preparedness even a partial mobilization would be if it were ordered, and still more a general mobilization, as in the first case a partial mobilization would render difficult a general mobilization if such should prove necessary subsequently.

After examining the situation from all points, both the Ministers and the Chief of the General Staff decided that in view of the small probability of avoiding a war with Germany it was indispensable to prepare for it in every way in good time, and that therefore the risk could not be accepted of delaying a general mobilization later by effecting a partial mobilization now. The conclusion arrived at at this conference was at once reported by telephone to the Tzar, who authorized the taking of steps accordingly. This information was received with enthusiasm by the small circle of those acquainted with what was in progress. Telegrams were at once dispatched to Paris and London to inform the respective Governments of the decision that had been come to.

At the same time the Imperial Ambassador in Paris was instructed to thank the French Government for the declaration made by the French Ambassador yesterday. The Imperial Ambassador in London was directed to address to the English Government a request "to range itself alongside of Russia and France without delay in order to prevent the European balance from being destroyed."

At about 11 p.m. the Minister for War informed the Foreign Minister by telephone that he had received orders from the Tzar to stop the general mobilization.

At about 1 a.m. the German Ambassador insistently requested the Minister to see him immediately, despite the lateness of the hour, on very pressing business. S. D. Sazonov, who had already gone to bed, rose and received the Ambassador, who asked if we could not be satisfied with an assurance on the part of Austria

HOW THE WAR BEGAN IN 1914

not to violate the integrity of Serbia. The Minister replied that this would not suffice, and at the pressing request of the Ambassador drew up and handed to Count Pourtalès the text of a formula which set forth the conditions on which Russia would be willing to cease her armed preparations.[1]

[1] This statement agrees with the French Yellow Book No. 103, and the English Blue Book, No. 97, but differs considerably from Pourtalès' corresponding communication. In reply to a question on the subject, Count Pourtalès stated as follows, on the 14th of February, 1924, to the Central Organization for inquiring into the origins of the war: "There is not the slightest doubt that my conversation with Sazonov, during which he set forth the formula, took place on the 30th of July during the midday hours. I remember it perfectly. My telegram concerning this conversation, published in vol. ii, p. 148, under No. 421 of the *German Documents*, was given out in Petersburg at 1.1 p.m., and begins with the words: 'In accordance with instructions, telegram No. 139, have just spoken with Sazonov.' This telegram No. 139 from the Imperial Chancellor, however, was only sent to the chief telegraph office in Berlin at 11 o'clock, and therefore could not possibly have been in my hands when I conversed with Sazonov during the night at about midnight. In fact, I only received it on the morning of the 30th of July. It formed the occasion for the conversation held at midday on the 30th of July, during which Sazonov, when urged by me, wrote out the formula.

"The conversation during the night of the 29th-30th of July was not, as is maintained in the latest Russian publications, of my seeking, but, on the contrary, it was Sazonov who requested me by telephone at midnight to come to him. This was some hours after I had communicated to him the contents, which he had heard with great excitement, of telegram No. 134 from Berlin (*German Documents*, vol. ii, p. 59, No. 342). Apparently Sazonov had meanwhile spoken with the Tzar, who in consequence of a telegram received from Kaiser Wilhelm, he had found to be less inclined for war than he himself had become during the last few days."

During the day small, and subsequently larger, crowds appeared in the streets carrying portraits of the Tzar and the national flag, and singing the hymn " Save Thy people, Lord." The demonstrators stopped before the Winter Palace, and also before the War Office and the Foreign Office.

A third [1] interview of the German Ambassador with the Minister at 2 a.m. Deeply disturbed and agitated at the prospect of the inevitability of a European war, Count Pourtalès insistently requested the Minister to formulate some proposal which he could telegraph to his Government.[2] The Minister drew up and handed to the Ambassador the following formula :—

" If Austria, recognizing that her conflict with Serbia has assumed the character of a question of general European interest, declares herself ready to eliminate from her ultimatum those items which violate the principle of Serbian sovereignty, Russia undertakes to cease all her military preparations." [3]

[1] A second variant of the note regarding the third interview of the German Ambassador with the Minister is given in the diary on the right side of the page, but without any reference as to its having been published in any way officially.—ED.

[2] The variants of the entry in the diary concerning the third meeting of the German Ambassador with the Minister is given on the right-hand page of the diary, but without anything to show whether this was officially published in any way.

[3] The wording of the text as reproduced here does not agree with the original text which is in the possession of Count Pourtalès. The original formula was as follows : " Si l'Autriche déclare qu'en reconnaissant que son conflit avec la Serbie a assumé le caractère d'une question d'interêt européen, se déclare prête à éliminer de son ultimatum les points qui portent atteinte aux droits souverains de la Serbie, la Russie s'engage à cesser tous préparatifs militaires."

TELEGRAM No. 1541 TO BUKHAREST.

The object of our possible action against Austria is not to permit the destruction of Serbia. We do not exclude the possibility of advantages for Rumania if she will participate in a war against Austria.

SAZONOV.

TELEGRAM No. 1543 TO STOCKHOLM AND BUKHAREST.

It is desirable to know whether the King of Sweden (Rumania) has received the German or Austrian Ambassador in audience.

SAZONOV.

TELEGRAM No. 1544 TO BERLIN, VIENNA, ROME, NISCH, LONDON, PARIS, BUKHAREST AND CONSTANTINOPLE.

The German Ambassador states that Germany continues to exercise a moderating influence in Vienna. I informed the Ambassador that our military measures were not directed against Germany, neither do they imply a decision to take action against Austria. At the Ambassador's instance, I expressed readiness to continue direct representations in Vienna and to proceed to a conference of the four Powers.

TELEGRAM No. 1547 TO LONDON, PARIS AND NISCH.

Communicate Telegram No. 1544 to the Governments concerned.

SAZONOV.

TELEGRAM NO. 1548 TO PARIS, LONDON, VIENNA, BERLIN, ROME, CONSTANTINOPLE, BUKHAREST AND NISCH.

In view of Shebeko's telegram No. 105, we leave the initiative entirely to England.

SAZONOV.

TELEGRAM NO. 1551 TO LONDON AND PARIS.

The German Ambassador has announced Germany's decision to mobilize if Russia does not cease to arm. It only remains for us to hasten our armed preparation and to reckon with the inevitably of war.

SAZONOV.

TELEGRAM NO. 1552 TO BERLIN AND SOFIA.[1]

Communication of military information by our Consuls.

SAZONOV.

TELEGRAM NO. 3 OF THE TZAR TO KAISER WILHELM.[2]

Thanks for your telegram conciliatory and friendly, whereas official message presented to-day by your Ambassador to my Minister was conveyed in a very different tone. Beg you to explain this divergency. It would be right to give over the Austro-Servian

[1] See telegram No. 1504 in the appendix.
[2] After the heading there is added in pencil the following: "According to information obtained from the Chief of the Department of Posts and Telegraphs, this was sent off at 8.20 p.m." Beneath the text of the telegram there is added in ink: "Given out 16/29 July at 8.20 p.m. at Peterhof. No. 168."

problem to The Hague Conference so as to prevent bloodshed. Trust in your wisdom and friendship.

TELEGRAM NO. 4 OF KAISER WILHELM TO THE TZAR.[1]
BERLIN, 6.35 P.M. RECEIVED 9.20 P.M.

I received your telegram and share your wish that peace should be maintained, but, as I told you, I cannot consider Austria's action against Servia as an ignoble war. Austria knows by experience that Servian promises on paper are wholly unreliable. I understand Austria's action must be judged as trending to have full guarantees that the Servian promises shall become real facts. This reasoning of mine is borne out by the statement of the Austrian Cabinet that Austria does not want to make any territorial conquests at the expense of Servia. I therefore suggest that it would be quite possible for Russia to remain a spectator of the Austro-Servian conflict without involving Europe in the most horrible war she ever witnessed. I think a direct understanding between your Government and Vienna possible and desirable, and, as I already telegraphed to you, my Government is continuing its exertions to promote it. Of course, military measures on the part of Russia which could be looked upon by Austria as threatening would precipitate a calamity we both wish to avoid, and jeopardize my position as mediator which I readily accepted on your appeal to my friendship and my help.

[1] To this there follows the following addition in pencil: "This reply telegram from Kaiser Wilhelm has caused His Majesty to cancel the decision regarding general mobilization."
Under the text of the telegram is the addition in ink: "Dispatched 16/19 July from Neues Palais at 6.35 p.m., delivered at Peterhof 9.40 p.m. No. 65."—ED.

The reply to telegram No. 2 was dispatched by Kaiser Wilhelm at 6.35 p.m., and received by His Majesty at 9.40 p.m.[1]

Telegram No. 5[2] from the Tzar to Kaiser Wilhelm.

Thank you heartily for your quick answer. Am sending Tatistchev this evening with instructions. The military measures which have now come into force were decided five days ago for reasons of defence on account of Austria's preparations. I hope from all my heart that these measures won't in any way interfere with your part as mediator, which I greatly value. We need your strong pressure on Austria to come to an understanding with us.

Sverbeev's Note.[3]

On returning to Berlin on Wednesday, 16/29 July, 1914, I went to the French Ambassador, M. Jules

[1] There is the following further addition in pencil: "This reply from the Emperor Wilhelm caused His Majesty to alter his decision regarding general mobilization."

[2] Under the text the following is added in pencil: "According to the White Book this telegram was dispatched at 1.20 a.m. on the 17th of July."
Beneath the text of this telegram the following words are added in pencil: "According to the White Book, this telegram was sent off at 1.20 p.m. on the 17th of July"; and in ink: "Given out at Peterhof 17/30 July at 1.20 a.m., No. 174."—Ed.

[3] The note of S. Sverbeev, the former Russian Ambassador in Berlin, is broken up into parts which are placed in the diary on the days to which they severally refer and are similarly placed in the Russian translation. For the original French text see the appendix.—Ed.

Cambon, who said to me that, in his opinion, the situation was very serious and that there was scarcely any hope of a peaceful issue. He added that at any rate, judging by a telegram from his brother Paul Cambon, the French Ambassador in London, in consequence of the refusal of the Vienna Cabinet to accept the more than conciliatory reply of Servia to the Austro-Hungarian ultimatum, France and Russia were assured of the actual support of England in the event of war.

Having acquainted myself with the contents of the telegram in question, which I did not find so convincing as my French colleague had stated it to be, I went to Sir E. Goschen and asked him what was England's attitude towards the present acute European crisis.

Not receiving any precise reply to my question, I set forth to my English colleague my point of view, and added that having regard to the conviction existing in Germany that in the event of an armed conflict between Germany and Austria on the one side, and Russia and France on the other, England would maintain strict neutrality, *it entirely depended upon the latter* whether the one or the other way out of the present situation would be adopted. If Sir Edward Grey *plainly and categorically* declared to Berlin that Great Britain was firmly determined to co-operate with Russia and France, *then peace was assured*. The English Ambassador replied that he did not know the intentions of his Government, and in spite of all that I advanced in support of my argument I received no satisfactory answer from him.

My first interview with the Secretary of State took place at 5 p.m. As I entered, von Jagow said to me: "The circumstances under which we again meet are sad, very sad"; to which I replied: "You wished it so."

After that I repeated to the Secretary of State the conversation I had with Herr Zimmermann on the day following the Serajevo crime, during which I directed his attention to the fact that Austria-Hungary had no right to throw upon all Serbia the responsibility for the assassination of the Archduke Franz Ferdinand, which was planned *in Austria by Austrian subjects.* If the Vienna Cabinet really intended, as Herr Zimmermann had given me to understand was the case, to demand that Serbia should conduct an investigation for the purpose of establishing the guilt of these subjects and obtaining the punishment of the guilty should they be discovered, the Vienna Cabinet would have been well advised not to present this request to Serbia in the form of an official note but by means of a friendly discussion with the representative of the neighbour kingdom which I had no doubt, but indeed maintained, would have manifested the utmost correctness with regard to this request, the more so because her own interests (her vital interests) were concerned in coming, after her victorious war, to an understanding with Austria regarding the economic questions which affected these two neighbouring States.

With regard to the Austrian ultimatum, I continued, it was unacceptable to Serbia, and Austria-Hungary knew this quite well. Consequently she desired war. In addition she knew that Russia could not remain inactive in presence of this armed collision. But what astonished me most, I said to the Secretary of State, was that Germany, who was acquainted with the terms of this ultimatum and who knew that we could not allow Serbia to be *crushed* or *weakened*, should approve of it. It was evident that she also was not averse to war.

Herr von Jagow replied that he had known nothing concerning the ultimatum, besides which this was a matter which exclusively concerned Austria-Hungary and Serbia (*re* the Serbian propaganda and the assassination of the Archduke), whereupon I exclaimed: " In that case you allow complete liberty of action to your ally."

Without replying to this observation, the Secretary of State answered that the Habsburg Monarchy sought neither the destruction of the neighbour State nor territorial annexations, but merely contemplated a punitory expedition. Moreover, he said, the Serbian affair in no way concerned Russia, and he, Jagow, could not recognize the rôle assumed by Russia of official protector of the Balkans. "If this were allowed, Germany had an equal right with regard to the small Protestant States—for example, Sweden." It will be understood that I protested energetically against this argument, which was really no argument. With regard to territorial annexations, I added, it was possible that Austria-Hungary did not desire any at the present moment, but that I knew only too well how wars were waged and how capable they were of bringing about unexpected results. I did not doubt for a moment that Austria had firmly decided to take possession of the Sandjak, for ceding which in 1898 (1908 ?) [1] she could not up to the present forgive

[1] This is as written in the original. Manifestly the second date, viz. 1908, is the correct one. It was then that Austria withdrew her troops from the Novi Bazar sandjak and in accordance with a convention concluded with Turkey on the 26th of February, 1909, renounced the rights accorded to her by the Treaty of Berlin and the Constantinople agreement of the 26th of April, 1879.—ED.

herself, in order to separate Serbia from Montenegro. Although the Austrian ultimatum was unacceptable, I continued, Serbia had agreed to eight or nine points, and had astonished all Europe by her conciliatory attitude. For its part the Habsburg Monarchy ought to have been satisfied with this surprising reply.

"That was impossible," replied Herr von Jagow, "because in this reply there was much left out which ought to have been referred to, and because the promises contained in it are not sincere." I protested energetically, and remarked that no one had the right to doubt Serbia's honesty.

After that I passed on to Sir E. Grey's proposal which Germany had rejected but which, although perhaps wanting in some respects, nevertheless offered a means of salvation because it opened the way for deliberations, while Germany's proposal for conversations between the cabinets would have been much more complicated. At critical moments such as we were now experiencing we must profit by every ray of hope, because time would not wait, and it was a case of minutes, not of days or even hours.

"Germany did not reject the English proposal," answered von Jagow, "but considered it purposeless. It would be better to hold conversations between the Cabinets. For the rest," he added, "it would be impossible that four Powers should constitute themselves an areopagus to sit in judgment upon two other Powers." Thereupon I observed that one of these Great Powers (Russia) had agreed to this course and that it was again Austria-Hungary who had declined to participate in the conference proposed by Grey because, as usual, she did not wish to make concessions. I added that under the circumstances the situation appeared to me as serious as could be and threatened to have most dangerous consequences.

At this moment a paper was brought to Herr von Jagow, which he read with "horror," and then handed it to me, asking me if the information set forth in it was true. It referred to our mobilization against Austria-Hungary of which I had been authorized to inform him. I confirmed this information and, in accordance with my instructions, emphasized the fact that *this was not a hostile measure with respect to Germany*, and added that Russia had all the more reason for mobilizing on the Austrian frontier because, according to information which I had received from a reliable source, Austria was making extensive military preparations in Galicia.

Herr von Jagow denied these preparations and said that, in view of our mobilization against Austria-Hungary, Germany must also mobilize, and that therefore there was nothing more to do but that from now onwards the diplomats must speak through the cannon's mouth.

I could not conceal from von Jagow my astonishment at this remark, in that no farther back than on the preceding day he had told Cambon that our mobilization against Austria did not involve mobilization by Germany against us. Herr von Jagow replied, evidently in great confusion: "But having learned that Russia is preparing to concentrate troops on the frontier of Germany, the latter is, of course, obliged to mobilize also."

I replied that I knew nothing at all as to what we were doing, but doubted whether this intelligence was true. With regard to Germany, I had precise and credible information that she was doing nothing less than concentrating her forces against us.

Herr von Jagow[1] energetically protested against these alleged preparations, and endeavoured, entirely without success, to persuade me that only officers who were on leave and troops which had been taking part in the manœuvres had been recalled. (The occupation of Luxembourg by Germany with 100,000 troops on the day following the declaration of war affords illuminating proof to the contrary.[2])

17/30 JULY.

Between 9 and 10 a.m. the Minister for Foreign Affairs spoke to the Minister for Agriculture by telephone. Both of them were greatly disturbed at the stoppage of the general mobilization, as they fully realized that this threatened to place Russia in an extremely difficult position in the event of relations with Germany becoming acute. S. D. Sazonov advised A. V. Krivoshein to beg an audience of the Tzar in order to represent to His Majesty the dangers called forth by the change.

At 11 a.m. the Minister for Foreign Affairs again met the Minister for War and the Chief of the General Staff. Information received during the night still further strengthened the opinion which they all held that it was imperative to prepare for a serious war

---

[1] Jagow's conversation with Cambon had taken place as early as the 27th of July. See French Yellow Book No. 67.

[2] Luxemburg was not occupied by a corps of 100,000 men, but by the 16th Infantry Division *at peace strength* on the 2nd of August, i.e. the day after the declaration of war against Russia and the first day of the German mobilization. On the evening of the 3rd of August this force was joined by the 3rd Cavalry Division and the 5th Composite Infantry Brigade, which had carried out " accelerated " (i.e. had not attained full war strength) mobilization and which belonged to the frontier defence force.

without loss of time. Accordingly the Ministers and the Chief of the Staff adhered to the view which they had expressed yesterday to the effect that it was indispensable to proceed to a general mobilization. Adjutant-General Sukhomlinov and General Yanushkevich again endeavoured by telephone to persuade the Tzar to revert to his decision of yesterday to permit a general mobilization. His Majesty decidedly refused to do so, and finally shortly declared that the conversation was at an end. General Yanushkevich, who at this moment was holding the telephone receiver, only succeeded in reporting that the Minister for Foreign Affairs was there with him and asked to be allowed to say a few words to His Majesty. A somewhat lengthy silence ensued, after which the Tzar expressed his willingness to hear the Minister. S. D. Sazonov requested His Majesty to receive him to-day, to enable him to present a report concerning the political situation which admitted of no delay. After a silence, the Tzar asked: "Is it all the same to you if I receive you at 3 o'clock, at the same time as Tatistchev, as otherwise I have not a free minute to-day?" The Minister thanked His Majesty and said that he would present himself at the hour named.

The Chief of the Staff warmly pleaded with S. D. Sazonov to persuade the Tzar without fail to consent to a general mobilization in view of the extreme danger that would result for us if we were not ready for war with Germany should circumstances demand the taking of decisive measures by us after the success of a general mobilization had been compromised by recourse to a partial mobilization. General Yanushkevich requested the Minister that in the event of his succeeding in persuading the Tzar he would telephone to him to that effect from Peterhof, in order that he might immediately take the necessary steps, as it would be requisite first of all to stop as soon as possible the partial mobilization which had already commenced and substitute fresh orders for those which had been issued. "After that," said Yanushkevich, "I shall go away, smash my telephone and generally adopt measures which will prevent anyone from finding me for the purpose of giving contrary orders which would again stop our general mobilization."

On his return to the Foreign Office, S. D. Sazonov had an interview with the French Ambassador.

Meanwhile A. V. Krivoshein informed S. D. Sazonov that in reply to his request that the Tzar would receive him he was told that His Majesty was so extremely occupied to-day that he could not see him. Krivoshein then expressed a desire to see S. D. Sazonov before the latter went to Peterhof. It was decided that they should breakfast together at Donon's, and at 12.30 they and Baron Schilling met in a private room there. The general state of mind was tense and the conversation was almost exclusively concerned with the necessity for insisting upon a general mobilization at the earliest possible moment, in view of the inevitableness of war with Germany, which momentarily became clearer. A. V. Krivoshein expressed the hope that S. D. Sazonov would succeed in persuading the Tzar, as otherwise, to use his own words, we should be marching towards a certain catastrophe.

At 2 p.m. the Minister for Foreign Affairs left for Peterhof, together with Major-General Tatistchev, and both of them were received together there in the Alexander Palace by His Majesty. During the course of nearly an hour the Minister proceeded to show that war was becoming inevitable, as it was clear to everybody that Germany had decided to bring about a collision, as otherwise she would not have rejected all the pacificatory proposals that had been made and could easily have brought her ally to reason. Under these circumstances it only remained to do everything that was necessary to meet war fully armed and under the most favourable conditions for ourselves. Therefore it was better to put away any fears that our warlike preparations would bring about a war, and to continue these preparations carefully rather than by reason of such fears to be taken unawares by war.

The firm desire of the Tzar to avoid war at all costs, the horrors of which filled him with repulsion, led His Majesty in his full realization of the heavy responsibility which he took upon himself in this fateful hour to explore every possible means for averting the approaching danger. Consequently he refused during a long time to agree to the adoption of measures which, however, indispensable from a military point of view, were calculated, as he clearly saw, to hasten a decision in an undesirable sense.

The tenseness of feeling experienced by the Tzar at this time found expression, amongst other signs, in the irritability most unusual with him, with which His Majesty interrupted General Tatistchev. The latter, who throughout had taken no part in the conversation, said in a moment of silence: "Yes, it is hard to decide." His Majesty replied in a rough and displeased tone: "I will decide"—in order by this means to prevent the General from intervening any further in the conversation.

Finally the Tzar agreed that under the existing circumstances it would be very dangerous not to make timely preparations for what was apparently an inevitable war, and therefore gave his decision in favour of an immediate general mobilization.

S. D. Sazonov requested the Imperial permission to inform the Chief of the General Staff of this immediately by telephone, and this being granted, he hastened to the telephone on the ground floor of the palace. Having transmitted the Imperial order to General Yanushkevich, who was waiting impatiently for it, the Minister, with reference to their conversation that morning, added: "Now you can smash your telephone."

Meanwhile His Majesty still cherished the hope of finding some means of preventing the general mobilization from becoming an irrevocable *casus belli*. To this end the Tzar, in a telegram dispatched to the Kaiser Wilhelm on this same day regarding the decision come to, gave his solemn word that despite the mobilization referred to . . .

(NOTE.—In the original this sentence remains unfinished. For N. Romanov's telegram see below.)

TELEGRAM NO. 1554, NOS. 1 AND 2 TO BERLIN.

The German Ambassador has asked whether we could not be satisfied with Austria's promise not to violate the integrity of Serbia. I replied that this would not suffice, and, at the pressing request of the Ambassador, dictated to him our conditions.

SAZONOV.

TELEGRAM NO. 1555 TO BERLIN, PARIS, LONDON AND VIENNA.

Until we receive a satisfactory reply from Austria, we shall continue our military preparations.

SAZONOV.

TELEGRAM No. 1556 TO BUKHAREST.

We are ready to support the annexation of Transylvania to Rumania.

SAZONOV.

TELEGRAM No. 1558 TO LONDON.

Concerning the Turkish ships under construction in England.

SAZONOV.

TELEGRAM No. 6 FROM THE EMPEROR WILHELM TO THE TZAR.[1] DISPATCHED 3.52 P.M. RECEIVED 5.30 P.M.

Best thanks for telegram. It is quite out of question that my Ambassador's language could have been in contradiction with the tenor of my telegram. Count Pourtalès was instructed to draw the attention of your Government to the danger and grave consequences involved by your mobilization. I said the same in my telegram to you. Austria has only mobilized against Servia, and only a part of her army. If, as it is now the case, according to the communication by you and your Government, Russia mobilizes against Austria, my rôle as mediator you kindly entrusted me with, and which I accepted at your express prayer, will be endangered if not ruined. The whole weight of the decision lies solely on your shoulders now, who have to bear the responsibility for peace or war.

[1] Under the text of the telegram there is written in pencil: "According to the White Book, dispatched at 1 a.m."; and in ink: "Given out in Berlin 17/30 July, 1914, at 3.52 p.m. Delivered at Peterhof at 6.30 p.m. No. 633."

REPORT BY SVERBEEV.

Thursday, 3 p.m.[1] The *Lokal Anzeiger* announces mobilization by Germany (my cypher telegram).

3.10 p.m. Dementi by the Wolff agency (my open telegram).

3.15 p.m. Excuses and dementi by Jagow (my second cypher telegram).

In the evening, not having then received telegram No. 2 containing our counter proposals to the proposal of the Berlin Cabinet, at 11.30 I went to the Secretary of State to ascertain what he knew about the matter.

Herr von Jagow informed me that he had received a telegram from Count Pourtalès, and having run through this long message, he read out to me from it an extract including the text of the formula proposed by us which fully corresponded with what I received the next morning.

I said to von Jagow that the Berlin Cabinet ought to accept our proposal, which was acceptable in all respects, the more so because Serbia, surprisingly enough, had agreed to eight or nine points of the Austro-Hungarian ultimatum.

The Secretary of State replied that this was impossible and that the Habsburg Monarchy would not *humiliate itself and deal a blow at its own prestige.*

I retorted that the prestige of a Great Power could not be shaken by such a concession; that we were endeavouring by every means to preserve peace; that

---

[1] Continuation of Sverbeev's note. In the original, above the words "3 p.m." there is written in pencil: "2.30 p.m."; above 3.10 p.m. is written: "2.40"; and above 3.15: "2.45."

Germany and Austria for their part did not wish to do anything towards this end; and that after the bombardment of Belgrade, which constituted a satisfaction for Austria, the latter ought to manifest more conciliatoriness. I added that the situation was becoming *more and more dangerous*. But everything that I said to von Jagow failed to change his point of view.

18/31 JULY.

To avoid rendering more acute our relations with Germany the Minister for Foreign Affairs deemed it desirable to proceed to the general mobilization as far as possible secretly and without making any public announcement concerning it. However, it appeared that this was impossible in a technical sense, and from the forenoon of the 18th of July announcements appeared in every street, printed on red paper, summoning men to the colours.

This could not but cause excitement among the foreign representatives, and one of the first of them who came to the Foreign Minister was the German Ambassador. S. D. Sazonov informed him that the decision taken by the Imperial Government merely constituted a precautionary measure necessitated by the unconciliatoriness manifested in Berlin and Vienna, and that Russia for her part would do nothing that was irrevocable, but that, despite her mobilization, peace could be maintained if Germany would consent before it was too late to exercise a moderating influence upon her ally.

Count Pourtalès did not conceal his fears as to the reception that would be accorded to the measure in question by Berlin.

NOTE HANDED BY THE GERMAN AMBASSADOR, ON THE 18TH OF JULY, 1914, TO A. A. NERATOV, THE ASSISTANT TO THE MINISTER FOR FOREIGN AFFAIRS.

In order to prove its pacificatory attitude and its friendly disposition towards Russia, and recognizing the difficulty of the latter's position in consequence of Austria's action with regard to Serbia, the German Government proposed to the Vienna Cabinet to give assurances to the Government in Petersburg to the effect that it had no intention of violating the territorial integrity of Serbia or of interfering with the legitimate interests of Russia.

In consequence of the advice proffered by Germany to Vienna, Austria made a declaration which, in the opinion of the German Government, should suffice to reassure Russia. A declaration of this kind, by which a Great Power when in a state of war binds its own hands in advance in order to conclude peace, must be regarded as a very substantial concession and as a proof of its desire for peace.

Russia should take into consideration that in endeavouring to oblige Austria to go farther than this declaration, she asks the latter to do something which is not consonant with the dignity and prestige of a Great Power. In reproaching Austria for violating the sovereign rights of Serbia, Russia herself violates those of Austria.

The Russian Government ought not to lose sight of the fact that *Germany is interested* in maintaining the prestige of Austria as a Great Power, and that it cannot be demanded of Germany that she should bring pressure to bear on Austria in a direction which is opposed to Germany's own interests.

HOW THE WAR BEGAN IN 1914

Under these circumstances, if Russia insists upon her demands and refuses to recognize the localization of the Austro-Serbian conflict, as it is absolutely indispensable that she should in the interests of the peace of Europe, she ought at the same time to become perfectly clear as to the extreme gravity of the situation.

TELEGRAM No. 1574 TO NISCH.

Does not Serbia consider this the proper time for an agreement with Bulgaria as regards military co-operation in exchange for territorial compensation supposing Serbia also obtained such compensation elsewhere?

SAZONOV.

TELEGRAM No. 1576 TO CONSTANTINOPLE.

In reply to our question regarding military preparations by Turkey, Fachreddin expressed ignorance concerning them and asked us regarding our military preparations in the Caucasus. We explained to him that these need not cause Turkey anxiety.

SAZONOV.

TELEGRAM No. 1579 TO BUKHAREST.

Personal.

TELEGRAM No. 1583 TO PARIS, LONDON, BERLIN, VIENNA AND ROME.

At the instance of the British Government I have replied agreeing to certain alterations in the formula which I proposed to the German Ambassador yesterday.

SAZONOV.

Telegram No. 1582 to Paris, London, Berlin and Rome.

Formula amended conformably to the English proposal. Text of formula follows.

Telegram No. 1587 to Nisch.

A credit of twenty million francs opened for Serbia.

Telegram No. 1589 to London and Paris.

I requested the British Ambassador to convey to Grey our recognition of the friendly and firm tone of England.

SAZONOV.

Telegram No. 1592 to Berlin, Vienna, Paris, London and Rome.

The Austrian Ambassador has visited me and communicated the consent of his Government to reconsider the ultimatum. I drew the Ambassador's attention to the fact that it would be preferable to conduct the negotiations in London with all the Great Powers participating in them. It is very desirable that Austria should cease military operations on Serbian territory.

SAZONOV.

Telegram No. 7 from the Tzar to Kaiser Wilhelm.[1]

PETERHOF.

I thank you heartily for your mediation, which begins to give one hope that all may yet end peace-

[1] Beneath the text of this telegram there is written in ink: "Given out at Peterhof 18/31 July at 2.55 p.m. Handed in at Berlin at 3.28 p.m. No. 189."—ED.

HOW THE WAR BEGAN IN 1914 73

fully. It is technically impossible to stop our military preparations, which were obligatory owing to Austria's mobilization. We are far from wishing war. As long as the negotiations with Austria on Serbia's account are taking place my troops shall not make any provocative actions. I give you my solemn word for this. I put all my trust in God's mercy and hope in your successful mediation in Vienna for the welfare of our countries and for the peace of Europe.

TELEGRAM No. 8 FROM KAISER WILHELM TO THE TZAR.[1]

BERLIN, NEW PALACE, 2.15 P.M. RECEIVED AT PETERHOF AT 5.35 P.M.

HIS MAJESTY THE TZAR.

On your appeal to my friendship and your call for assistance I began to mediate between your and the Austro-Hungarian Government. While this action was still proceeding your troops were mobilized against Austria-Hungary, my ally, thereby, as I have already pointed out to you, my mediation has been made almost illusory. I nevertheless have continued my action. I now receive authentic news of serious preparations for war on my eastern frontier. Responsibility for the safety of my empire forces preventive measures of defence upon me. In my endeavours to maintain the peace of the world I have gone to the utmost limit possible. The responsibility for the disaster which is now threatening the whole civilized world will not be laid at my door. In this moment

[1] Under the text of this telegram there is written in ink: "Given out at the Neues Palais 18/31 July, 2.15 p.m. Delivered at Peterhof 5.15 p.m. No. 148."

it still lies in your power to avert it. Nobody is threatening the honour or power of Russia, who can well afford to await the result of my mediation. My friendship for you and your empire, transmitted to me by my grandfather on his death-bed, has always been sacred to me, and I have honestly often backed up Russia when she was in serious trouble, especially in the last war. The peace of Europe may still be maintained by you if Russia will agree to stop the military measures which must threaten Germany and Austria-Hungary.

Note by S. Sverbeev.

The following day, Friday, at 10 a.m., I renewed this conversation with the Secretary of State, endeavouring by every means to persuade him to accept our formula and to bring pressure to bear on the Vienna Cabinet in that sense, so as to induce the latter to relinquish those points in its ultimatum which were damaging to Serbian sovereignty. I added that any prolongation of the negotiations bringing advantage to Austria alone was *inadmissible*, as I observed that if, while we were exerting all our efforts to avoid a European war, neither Germany nor her ally desired to make any concessions (they have declined Grey's proposal and Germany will not accept our formula), then *war is inevitable*.

I encountered stubborn opposition from the Secretary of State, who gave me the same reply as yesterday—a reply which convinced me of the uselessness of any further conversations.

At 2 p.m. Herr von Jagow requested me to come to him, and on the basis of a telegram received from Count Pourtalès, informed me of our general mobiliza-

HOW THE WAR BEGAN IN 1914 75

tion, adding that *after this there was nothing more to be done*, that the Imperial and Royal Government was under the necessity of proclaiming at once that the fatherland was in danger and of issuing orders for general mobilization in Germany.

I expressed some doubt as to the authenticity of this information (our general mobilization), as I had received no direct announcement of any kind concerning it.

Jagow again began to refer to the exchange of telegrams between our Sovereigns, and said that the Emperor Wilhelm, apparently at the request of my august monarch, had accepted the rôle of mediator and had even telegraphed to the Emperor Franz Joseph, and then " at this very moment you mobilize your whole army," he added.

I replied, as before, that not being informed regarding the exchange of telegrams between our Sovereigns, I could say nothing on that point, but that, on the contrary, I saw that Germany did not wish to do anything in the interests of peace. With regard to the Kaiser's telegram to the Emperor Franz Joseph, I was astonished that Herr von Jagow had not told me about it sooner, and asked whether St. Petersburg knew of it. He replied that he supposed (?) so from the telegram of the Emperor Wilhelm to my august Sovereign.

(During all our preceding conversations the Secretary of State had given me to understand that the Berlin Cabinet was not able to exercise influence in Vienna for the purpose of bringing about a more conciliatory attitude on the part of the Austro-Hungarian Government.)

When we parted, Herr von Jagow repeated that in consequence of our mobilization the situation was hopeless, to which I replied that as an optimist by nature I never employ the word "finished" until the end has really come, but that, speaking unreservedly, I could not see what more could be done to obviate war.

At 3 p.m. took place the solemn entry into Berlin of the Emperor Wilhelm and all the Imperial family, followed by a speech delivered by His Majesty from the balcony, in which he announced that war had been forced upon him.

At 11 p.m. I was brought a sheet containing the ultimatum presented to Russia. Similar sheets were being distributed in the streets.

19 July/1 August.

Between 4 and 5 p.m. Count Pourtalès called up Baron Schilling on the telephone and said that it was indispensable that he should see the Minister at once. Baron Schilling replied that at the present time S. D. Sazonov was in Elagin Island attending a council of Ministers, and promised to inform the Ambassador directly the Minister returned. This was done soon after 6 p.m., and Count Pourtalès promptly came to the Ministry. When S. D. Sazonov was informed of this, he gave up all hope, and said to Baron Schilling: "He will probably bring me the declaration of war."

On entering the Cabinet the German Ambassador asked whether the Imperial Government was agreeable to giving him a favourable reply to his note of yesterday. The Minister replied in the negative, adding that although the order for general mobilization could not be changed, Russia did not refuse to continue negotiations for the purpose of arriving at a peaceful issue out of the present situation. Count Pourtalès, who had arrived in a state of great anxiety, now began to manifest signs of increasing emotion. Drawing out of his pocket a folded paper, he once more addressed to the Minister his previous question, emphasizing as he did so the serious consequences to which the refusal of Russia to consent to Germany's demand regarding the cessation of mobilization must lead. S. D. Sazonov firmly and calmly again confirmed the reply which he had just given. With increasing emotion the Ambassador repeated his question a third time, when the Minister once more replied to him: "I have no other reply to give you" (" Je n'ai pas d'autre réponse à vous donner "). The Ambassador, deeply moved and drawing a deep breath, exclaimed with difficulty: "In that case, sir, I am instructed by my Government to hand you this note " (" En ce cas, Monsieur le Ministre, Je suis chargé par mon Gouvernement de vous remettre cette note "); and with trembling hands he presented to S. D. Sazonov a note containing a declaration of war which, as subsequently became apparent, contained, by reason of the carelessness of the German Embassy in Petersburg, two variants combined in one text. This detail, however, was only noticed later on, as at the moment when the note was presented the prime significance of the German declaration was so clear that the actual words did not matter.

The conversation between the Ambassador and the Minister took place while they were standing in the big cabinet, and after he had presented the note Count Pourtalès, losing all self-control, went to the window (the first from the corner) and, putting his hands to his head, began to weep and exclaimed: "I never could have believed that I should quit Petersburg under these conditions " (" Je n'aurais jamais cru que Je quitterais Pétersbourg dans ces conditions").

He then embraced the Minister and went away, asking that he might be informed at the Embassy concerning the arrangements made for his departure, as he himself was not capable at the present moment of talking about anything.

Immediately summoning A. A. Neratov and Baron Schilling to himself, the Minister informed them regarding the conversation which had just taken place and instructed them to acquaint everybody concerned at once, while he at the same time reported by telephone to the Emperor.

Baron Schilling, for his part, hastened to telephone to the President of the Council of Ministers, the Ministers of War and Marine, the Finance Minister, and likewise the French and English Ambassadors. At the same time corresponding telegrams were dispatched to our representatives abroad informing them of Germany's declaration of war with us.

Just then Baron Grunelius, the Bavarian Minister, came to Baron Schilling. He was manifestly greatly grieved at all that had happened, and most dissatisfied at having to leave Petersburg. He said to Baron Schilling: "I have come to see you to ask you what I ought to do. I have no special instructions from my Government, but I believe that I ought to follow the German Embassy. All that has happened is very sad and annoying. Do you think that I ought to see the Minister? I expect he is very busy at this time and that it would be better not to disturb him. I request you to tell him how troubled I am concerning all that has happened" (" Je viens vous voir pour vous demander ce que Je dois faire. Je n'ai pas d'instructions spéciales de mon Gouvernement mais Je crois que Je dois suivre l'ambassade d'Allemagne. C'est bien triste et bien ennuyeux, tout ce qui se passe.

Croyez-vous que Je doive voir le Ministre ? Je pense qu'il doit être tres occupé en ce moment-ci et qu'il vaut mieux ne pas le déranger. Vous voudrez bien lui dire combien Je suis désolé de tous ces événements").

Baron Grunelius asked to be informed as to what had been decided regarding the departure of the German Embassy, to whose movements he considered that he ought to conform.

After communicating with the military authorities, the Minister of Communications and the Police Department (the latter with regard to the question of passing across the frontier those who would have to accompany the German Ambassador), it was decided to furnish the German Ambassador and the Embassy personnel, the Consuls, the Bavarian Minister, and about eighty other German subjects, with a special train at 8 o'clock next morning at the Finland terminus to proceed to Germany via Sweden. Baron Schilling informed Baron Prittwitz, the Ambassador's secretary, who had been instructed by Count Pourtalès to see to this matter, to this effect. The Foreign Office for its part entrusted Radkevich, an official for special services, to superintend the careful carrying out of the proposed measures, and also to accompany the departing Ambassador to the terminus.

TELEGRAM No. 1601 TO PARIS, LONDON, BERLIN AND ROME.

At midnight the German Ambassador informed me that if within twelve hours we did not proceed to demobilize, not only against Germany but also against Austria, the German Government would issue the order to mobilize. In reply to my question whether this was equivalent to war, the Ambassador replied No, but that we were very near to it.

SAZONOV.

TELEGRAM No. 1603 TO STOCKHOLM.

We learn that the King informed the German Minister that in the event of a European war Sweden will range herself on the side of the Triple Alliance.

SAZONOV.

TELEGRAM No. 1604 TO SAN SEBASTIAN.

Concerning the placing of Russian subjects in Germany and Austria under the protection of the Spanish representatives.

SAZONOV.

TELEGRAM No. 1618 TO THE IMPERIAL REPRESENTATIVES ABROAD.

Germany has just declared war with us.

SAZONOV.

TELEGRAM No. 1622 TO VIENNA.

Up to the present we continue to be in diplomatic relations with Austria.

SAZONOV.

TELEGRAM No. 1624 TO VIENNA.

(NOTE.—In the original text the contents of the telegram are not given. See appendix.)

TELEGRAM No. 1627 TO PARIS AND LONDON.

Germany is evidently endeavouring to place upon us the responsibility for the rupture. His Majesty bound himself by his word given to the German Emperor that he would undertake no aggressive action whilst discussions with Austria continue. In face of such a guarantee Germany had no right to doubt that we would accept any peaceful way out compatible with the dignity and independence of Serbia.

SAZONOV.

TELEGRAM No. 9 OF THE TZAR TO THE EMPEROR WILHELM.

I received your telegram. Understand you are obliged to mobilize, but wish to have the same guarantee from you as I gave you, that the measures *do not* mean war and that we shall continue negotiating for the benefit of our countries and universal peace dear to all our hearts. Our long proved friendship must succeed, with God's help, in avoiding bloodshed. Anxiously, full of confidence await your answer.

NOTE BY S. SVERBEEV.

Saturday. General mobilization in Germany (army and navy), and declaration of war against Russia.

TELEGRAM NO. 10 FROM KAISER WILHELM TO THE ALL HIGHEST PRESENTED TO THE MINISTER FOR FOREIGN AFFAIRS DURING THE NIGHT OF THE 19TH–20TH OF JULY, 1914.[1]

(NOTE.—Below the text of the telegram there is added in ink the words: " Dispatched from Berlin on the 19th July/1st August at 10.45 p.m. Delivered in Petersburg at 1.55 p.m. No. 3055.")

In the opinion of the German Ambassador, who has just been asked by telephone, this telegram was probably sent before the declaration of war.

Berlin. Dispatched at 10.45 p.m.
Received. 1.15 a.m.

Thanks for your telegram. I yesterday pointed out to your Government the way by which alone war may be avoided. Although I requested an answer for noon to-day, no telegram from my Ambassador conveying an answer from your Government has reached me as yet. I therefore have been obliged to mobilize my army. Immediate, affirmative, clear and unmistakable answer from your Government is the only way to avoid endless misery. Until I have received this answer, alas! I am unable to discuss the subject of your telegram. As a matter of fact I must request you to immediately order your troops on no account to commit the slightest act of trespassing over our frontiers.

[1] The Kaiser's telegram was dispatched at 10.45 p.m. after the declaration of war (*German Documents*, No. 600). The telegram containing the declaration of war was sent at 12.52 p.m. (*German Documents*, No. 542).
At the end of this telegram there is written in ink: " Given out 19 July–1 August in Berlin at 10.45 p.m. Delivered at Peterhof 1.55 p.m., No. 3055."—ED.

HOW THE WAR BEGAN IN 1914

LETTER FROM COUNT POURTALÈS TO THE MINISTER FOR FOREIGN AFFAIRS. SUNDAY, 4.30 A.M.

DEAR MINISTER,

Whatever happens, I desire to dispatch the attached telegram to Berlin. Please be so good as to acquaint yourself with its contents and to inform me whether it accurately describes the situation. I send you the telegram *au clair*. If you consider it desirable to send it from the Foreign Office, please do so. Otherwise send it back to me at once with your approval.

Yours very faithfully,
(*Signed*) POURTALÈS.

NOTE BY S. SVERBEEV.

At 10.30 a.m. on Sunday an official of the Foreign Office brought me my passport and announced that my train would proceed via Wirballen (Verjbolovo).

At 11 o'clock I was informed that Her Majesty the Empress could not get to Wirballen, (?) and that my train also would be sent by some other route as yet unknown.

During the day news of the occupation of Luxemburg by an Army Corps numbering 100,000 men (8th Corps) which had been already mobilized.

After the speech of the Emperor Wilhelm at 6.15 p.m. on Friday any further negotiations became superfluous.

S. SVERBEEV.

APPENDIX I

SECRET TELEGRAM FROM THE MINISTER TO THE AMBASSADOR IN VIENNA. ST. PETERSBURG, 9/22 JULY, 1914. NO. 1475.

ACCORDING to rumours received here, Austria is evidently preparing to make various demands upon Belgrade in connection with the events at Serajevo. Be so good as to point out to the Minister for Foreign Affairs in a friendly but firm manner the dangerous consequences to which such a step might lead should it prove to be of a nature that was incompatible with the dignity of Serbia. From conversations held with the French Minister for Foreign Affairs it appears that France also is very anxious regarding the change that may take place in Austro-Serbian relations, and is not inclined to permit any unjustifiable humiliation of Serbia. The French Ambassador in Vienna has been instructed to advise moderation on the part of the Austro-Hungarian Government. According to our information, London also condemns the intention ascribed to Austria of causing international complications with regard to this matter, and the British Government has also instructed its representative in Vienna to express himself in this sense. I do not yet lose hope that reason will prevail over warlike tendencies in Vienna and that timely warnings on the part of the Great Powers will still serve to restrain Austria from irrevocable measures. Before addressing

Count Berchtold on this subject be so good as to discuss it with your French and English colleagues, but bear in mind that in order to avoid any undesirable intensification of the question the steps taken by yourself and the others should be neither in the nature of combined action nor simultaneous.

SAZONOV.

SECRET TELEGRAM TO THE CHARGÉ D'AFFAIRES IN BELGRADE, 11/14 JULY, 1914. NO. 1487.

Pressing. Personal. Please decipher (this) yourself. If Serbia is really in such a helpless condition as to leave no doubt regarding the result of an armed struggle with Austria, it would perhaps be better that in the event of an invasion by Austria the Serbs should make no attempt whatever to offer resistance, but should retire and, allowing the enemy to occupy their territory without fighting, appeal to the Powers. In this appeal the Serbs, after pointing out the difficulty of their position after (the recent) war during which they gained the recognition of Europe by their moderation, might allude to the impossibility of their maintaining an unequal struggle, and ask for the protection of the Powers based upon a sense of justice.

SAZONOV.

SECRET TELEGRAM OF THE FOREIGN MINISTER TO THE AMBASSADOR IN LONDON. ST. PETERSBURG, 12/25 JULY, 1914. NO. 1489.

In view of the present course of events, the attitude which England will adopt becomes of the highest importance. So long as it is possible to avert a European war, it is easier for England than for any other Power to exert a moderating influence upon Austria, as she is regarded in Vienna as being the most disinterested of the Powers and there is therefore a greater disposition to listen to her. Unfortunately, according to our information, Austria on the day prior to that on which she took action in Belgrade thought she was justified in hoping that she would meet with no opposition from England, and this expectation influenced Austria's decision to a certain degree. It is therefore very desirable that England should firmly and clearly make it understood that she considers Austria's action unjustified by the circumstances and extremely dangerous to European peace, the more so because she could easily obtain by peaceful means the satisfaction of those of her demands which are founded upon justice and are compatible with the dignity of Serbia.

In the event of the situation becoming more acute in a manner calling for corresponding action on the part of the Great Powers, we rely upon it that England will not delay to range herself definitely on the side of Russia and France in order to maintain that European balance for which she has always stood in the past and which in the event of Austria's victory will undoubtedly be broken.

SAZONOV.

SECRET TELEGRAM FROM THE MINISTER FOR FOREIGN AFFAIRS TO THE CHARGÉ D'AFFAIRES IN BELGRADE, 12TH JULY, 1914. No. 1494.

Pressing.

In view of the special position of England, regarding whose disinterestedness with respect to the present question there is no doubt, war between Austria and

Serbia might perhaps be yet averted if the Serbian Government addressed a request for mediation to the English Government, and if the latter would accept this rôle. You might speak to Pashich concerning this and convey this idea to him.

SAZONOV.

To the Ambassador in London.

I am telegraphing to Belgrade: text of (above?) telegram follows here. Should the Serbs take a step of this kind in London, please support them energetically.

SAZONOV.

Secret Telegram from the Minister for Foreign Affairs to the Ambassador in Constantinople, and the Ministers in Sofia and Bukharest, and the Chargé d'Affaires at Athens, 12th July, 1914. No. 1496.

From a secret source which inspires confidence it appears that negotiations are evidently in progress between Turkey, Bulgaria and Austria with regard to the possible-participation of the two first named in the approaching conflict. Please be good enough to obtain confirmation of this information, if possible, and to follow up this question carefully.

Additional Instructions for Bukharest and Athens.

... and confidentially draw the attention of the Government to which you are accredited to this.

SAZONOV.

HOW THE WAR BEGAN IN 1914

Aide Mémoire.

A telegram in the following sense has been sent to His Majesty's Representative at Belgrade:—

Sir E. Grey has urged on the German Ambassador in London that military action should not be precipitated by Austria.

It appears to Sir E. Grey that it is clearly incumbent on Serbia to express to Austria her concern and regrets that those implicated in the recent murder of the Archduke should include any Serbians holding official rank, however subordinate, and she should certainly promise to give the fullest satisfaction in the event of this charge being proved. The Serbian reply must for the rest be framed to meet the requirements of Serbian interests.

Sir E. Grey is not in a position to know whether on the expiry of the time limit military action by Austria would be averted by anything less than the unconditional acceptance of her demands. It appears to him that the only chance is not to offer a blank refusal to these demands, but before the time limit expires to accept as many of them as possible.

His Majesty's Representative at Belgrade has been instructed to consult with his Russian and French colleagues as to the advisability of communicating the above considerations to the Serbian Government.

The Serbian Minister in London has urgently pressed Sir E. Grey to give some indication of the views of His Majesty's Government, but without being acquainted with the action being taken at Belgrade by the French and Russian Governments, Sir E. Grey does not like to undertake the responsibility of advising the Serbian Government even to the extent indicated above, and certainly not any further.

St. Petersburg,
 July 12/25, 1914.

Secret Telegram from the Minister for Foreign Affairs to the Representatives at Vienna, Stockholm, Bukharest, Constantinople, Christiania and Copenhagen.[1] Dispatched on 13th July, 1914, under No. 1504.

Please furnish by telegraph all the information you possess concerning the completing to strength and the movements of the land forces, the fitting out and movements of naval forces and the warlike measures in general undertaken *in countries adjacent to us.* You are likewise instructed at the same time to direct all consular officers who are subordinate to you to telegraph to the Foreign Office all information of the same kind that they may possess.

Sazonov.

Secret Telegram from the Minister for Foreign Affairs to the Ambassador at Rome. Also communicated to London and Paris. 13th July, 1914. No. 1505.

Urgent.

We consider that Italy could play a part of prime importance as regards the maintenance of peace if

[1] This telegram was sent to the representatives in Berlin and Sofia 16/29 July, 1914, under No. 1552, with the following addition to Sofia: ' After the underlined portion add, " and in Bulgaria and Turkey."—Ed.

she would exert the necessary influence on Austria and adopt a negative attitude towards the conflict, as the latter cannot remain localized. It is desirable that you yourself should express it to be your opinion that it is impossible for Russia to abstain from going to Serbia's assistance.

SAZONOV.

SECRET TELEGRAM FROM THE MINISTER FOR FOREIGN AFFAIRS TO THE MINISTER AT BUKHAREST, 13TH JULY, 1914. NO. 1506.

Urgent. Confidential.

I request you to explain to Bratianu in the following sense : We are doing all we can to prevent a conflict between Austria and Serbia. Serbia on her part is manifesting all the moderation that is compatible with her dignity.

If, however, our efforts prove vain, it will scarcely be possible for us to remain neutral and leave Serbia to her fate. We suppose that all her sympathies and her hopes for the future will indicate to Rumania the solidarity of her interests with those of Serbia. If to-day Austria assails Serbia with an accusation of irredentism, the same fate will overtake Rumania to-morrow, or she will be obliged to renounce for ever the consummation of her national ideals.

In view thereof it is imperative for us to know as soon as possible what attitude Rumania will assume if a conflict proves inevitable, and also towards any possible attempts on the part of Bulgaria to profit by hostilities between Austria and Serbia.

SAZONOV.

SECRET TELEGRAM FROM THE MINISTER FOR FOREIGN AFFAIRS TO THE CHARGÉ D'AFFAIRES IN BERLIN, 14/27 JULY, 1914. NO. 1514.

Please communicate secretly to all our missions in Germany for compliance there with the instruction contained in telegram No. 1504.

SAZONOV.

SECRET TELEGRAM FROM THE MINISTER FOR FOREIGN AFFAIRS TO THE REPRESENTATIVES IN CONSTANTINOPLE, SOFIA AND BUKHAREST, 14TH JULY, 1914, NO. 1522.

Simultaneously with the report you are sending to the Minister for Foreign Affairs, be so good as to inform the Commander-in-Chief of the Black Sea Fleet at Sevastopol direct by telegraph of all you know concerning the fitting out and the movements of Turkish, Bulgarian and Rumanian forces, and the general naval and military situation in the Black Sea region. You are at the same time instructed to charge with the same obligation the Consuls under your jurisdiction.

SAZONOV.

SECRET TELEGRAM FROM THE MINISTER FOR FOREIGN AFFAIRS TO THE MINISTER AT CETTINJE, 14TH JULY, 1914. NO. 1523.

Your telegram No. 68 received.

For your information and guidance. Russia has advised Serbia not to depart from her conciliatory attitude but to express her readiness to satisfy the demands of Austria in so far as they are compatible with the independence of Serbia. The Serbian Government appears to have quite realized the necessity for such a mode of action. While there still remains hope that the endeavours of Russia and the other Powers will lead to successful results, Montenegro should likewise observe these waiting and conciliatory tactics.

If, however, Austria remains unappeasable and attacks Serbia, Russia will not remain indifferent to the fate of the latter.

We consider that at the present moment Montenegro must more than ever co-ordinate her policy with that of Serbia in this matter, which is of common interest to them both. Upon this depends the nature of Russia's future relations with Montenegro.

SAZONOV.

SECRET TELEGRAM TO THE CHARGÉ D'AFFAIRES AT BELGRADE, 14TH JULY, 1914. No. 1525.

Please transmit to H.H. Prince Alexander the following reply from H.M. the Tzar :—

In addressing me at this particularly difficult moment your Royal Highness is not deceived regarding the sentiments which I entertain towards him and my cordial sympathy with the Serbian people.

The present situation is attracting my most serious attention, and my Government is employing all its strength for the purpose of smoothing out the existing difficulties. I do not doubt that your Highness and the Royal Government will neglect nothing that will serve to facilitate this task and will do everything possible to find a solution which, without injuring the dignity of Serbia, would render it possible to avert the horrors of a new war.

While the least hope remains of avoiding bloodshed all our efforts should be directed to that end. If, despite our sincere desires, we do not succeed, Russia will not under any circumstances remain indifferent to the fate of Serbia.

SECRET TELEGRAM FROM THE MINISTER FOR FOREIGN AFFAIRS TO THE AMBASSADOR IN LONDON. COMMUNICATED ALSO TO THE AMBASSADOR IN PARIS. 15TH JULY, 1914. NO. 1528.

From conversations with the German Ambassador I form the impression that Germany rather favours Austria's unconciliatoriness. The Berlin Cabinet, which is in a position to stop the development of the crisis, is manifestly bringing no pressure to bear upon Germany's ally. Her Ambassador here regards Serbia's reply as unsatisfactory.

I consider Germany's attitude to be very disturbing and believe that England could more successfully than any other Power take steps in Berlin to exercise a certain pressure. Undoubtedly the key of the situation is in Berlin.

SAZONOV.

SECRET TELEGRAM TO THE MINISTER AT BUKHAREST.[1] ST. PETERSBURG, 15/28 JULY, 1914. NO. 1536.

Urgent. Personal.

Please decipher this yourself. We learn from a highly trustworthy source that the Rumanian Minister in Berlin, acting upon instructions received from the

[1] On the original there is the prearranged note signifying the approval of N. Romanov in blue pencil.—ED.

HOW THE WAR BEGAN IN 1914   95

King and evidently from Bratianu also, requested Jagow to keep him *au fait* regarding the course of events, in order that Rumania, in the event of a war into which Russia would be drawn, might prepare public opinion and make warlike preparations. Beldiman is said to have declared that if Rumania received assurances that Bulgaria will not attack her in the rear it will then be possible for Rumania to operate with all her forces against Russia. We do not wish to believe this information, because if it proves to be true it would convict Rumania of unexampled treachery. Please inquire carefully into this and telegraph immediately.

SAZONOV.

SECRET TELEGRAM FROM THE MINISTER FOR FOREIGN AFFAIRS TO THE AMBASSADOR IN CONSTANTINOPLE, 15TH JULY, 1914. No. 1537.

Your telegram No. 569 received.

You may explain to the Turkish Ministers confidentially that we are taking general precautionary measures purely because the general complications may affect some of the Balkan States.

SAZONOV.

SECRET TELEGRAM FROM THE MINISTER FOR FOREIGN AFFAIRS TO THE AMBASSADOR IN LONDON, 15TH JULY, 1914. No. 1538.

Received telegram from London, No. 211, and now refer to my telegram No. 1521.

In consequence of Austria's declaration of war against Serbia, my direct discussions with the Austrian Ambassador are manifestly purposeless. Action by

England for the purpose of mediating and immediately stopping military operations by Austria against Serbia is indispensable. Otherwise mediation will only serve as a pretext for delaying the settlement of the question and afford Austria meanwhile an opportunity for completely crushing Serbia.

SAZONOV.

SECRET TELEGRAM FROM THE MINISTER FOR FOREIGN AFFAIRS TO THE MINISTER AT BUKHAREST, 16TH JULY, 1914. NO. 1541.

Your telegram No. 169 received.

I request you to communicate the following to Bratianu :—

In the event of an actual armed collision between Austria and Serbia, we contemplate intervening in order to prevent the destruction of the latter. That constitutes the object of our war with Austria, should such prove unavoidable.

Having thus answered Bratianu's questions, please ask him categorically in your turn what attitude Rumania will adopt, at the same time giving him to understand that we do not preclude the possibility of advantages for Rumania if she participates with us in a war against Austria. We should like to know what are the views of the Rumanian Government itself in this connection.

SAZONOV.

SECRET TELEGRAM TO THE MINISTERS IN STOCKHOLM AND BUKHAREST, 16/29 JULY, 1914. NO. 1543.

In order to establish the correctness of certain information it is desirable to know whether there took place at Stockholm (Sinaia) last Saturday, July 12th, a reception at which the King could have spoken with the German Minister, or the Austrian Minister could have met the Princes and the statesmen of their respective countries.

SCHILLING.

SECRET TELEGRAM FROM THE MINISTER FOR FOREIGN AFFAIRS TO THE AMBASSADORS IN PARIS AND LONDON AND TO THE CHARGÉ D'AFFAIRES IN SERBIA, 16TH JULY, 1914. No. 1547.

Urgent. Reference to my telegram No. 1544.

I request you to bring the contents of this telegram confidentially to the notice of the Government to which you are accredited.

SAZONOV.

SECRET TELEGRAM FROM THE MINISTER FOR FOREIGN AFFAIRS TO THE AMBASSADORS IN PARIS AND LONDON. COMMUNICATED TO VIENNA, ROME, BERLIN, CONSTANTINOPLE, NISCH AND BUKHAREST. 16TH JULY, 1914. No. 1548.

Reference to my telegram No. 1544.

When I conversed with the German Ambassador I had not then received Shebeko's telegram No. 105, which makes it clear that the Vienna Cabinet declines to effect an exchange of ideas with us. In view of this we leave it entirely to England to take such steps as she deems to be effective.

SAZONOV.

SECRET TELEGRAM FROM THE MINISTER FOR FOREIGN AFFAIRS TO THE MINISTER IN BUKHAREST, 17TH JULY, 1914. No. 1556.

Your telegram No. 170 received. Reference to my telegrams Nos. 1536 and 1341

Very confidential. If you consider it possible to proceed to a more concrete definition of the advantages upon which Rumania can count if she participates in a war against Austria, you may expressly declare to Bratianu that we are prepared to support the annexation of Transylvania to Rumania.

SAZONOV.

SECRET TELEGRAM FROM THE MINISTER FOR FOREIGN AFFAIRS TO THE AMBASSADOR IN LONDON, 17TH JULY, 1914. No. 1558.

Under present circumstances it is of the highest importance for us that Turkey should not receive the two dreadnoughts, *Rio de Janeiro* and *Reshad*, now being constructed for her in England. The construction of these ships is so far advanced that the first named could be dispatched to Turkey within the next few weeks and the latter within a few months. Be so good as to point out to the English Government the immense importance of this matter for us, and energetically insist upon the retention of these two ships in England.

SAZONOV.

SECRET TELEGRAM FROM THE MINISTER FOR FOREIGN AFFAIRS TO THE CHARGÉ D'AFFAIRES IN SERBIA, 18TH JULY, 1914. No. 1576.

Your letter of 14th July received.

In reply to our question regarding Turkey's war preparations, Fachreddin replied that he knew nothing concerning them, and in his turn asked a question regarding our military preparations in the Caucasus. We explained to him that at the present time we were adopting certain measures everywhere which, however, need not in any way disturb Turkey, and that it entirely depended upon the latter herself whether we remained on the best of relations with her.

SAZONOV.

SECRET TELEGRAM TO THE MINISTER AT BUKHAREST.[1]
ST. PETERSBURG, 18/31 JULY, 1914. No. 1579.

Personal.

Very confidential. We have positive information as to the possibility of military action by Rumania together with Austria against us. Without making it appear that our confidence in her is shaken, please be ready for any eventualities and take steps for the safe preservation of the secret archives by sending them in good time to Odessa. Judging by certain signs, there is still a possibility of ensuring that Rumania will not intervene or even that she will openly come over to our side as a result of the promise on our part of a corresponding compensation. As such we would agree to promise our support as regards the acquisition of Transylvania by Rumania. Please make a cautious explanation to this effect and telegraph your observations with regard to the matter to us.

SAZONOV.

[1] On the original there is the prearranged note signifying the approval of N. Romanov in blue pencil.—ED.

SECRET TELEGRAM FROM THE MINISTER FOR FOREIGN AFFAIRS TO THE CHARGÉ D'AFFAIRES AT NISCH, 18TH JULY, 1914. NO. 1587.

Your telegram No. 253 received.

The Serbian Minister here conveyed to us a request from Pashich to open a three-months' credit of 20 million francs, which our Minister of Finance has agreed to do.

SAZONOV.

SECRET TELEGRAM FROM THE MINISTER FOR FOREIGN AFFAIRS TO THE AMBASSADOR IN LONDON. COMMUNICATED TO PARIS. 18TH JULY, 1914. NO. 1589.

I requested the British Ambassador to convey to Grey our sincerest thanks for the friendly and firm tone adopted by him in the negotiations with Germany and Austria, thanks to which the hope of a peaceful issue out of the present situation is not yet lost.

I also asked him to inform the English Minister that I consider that only negotiations conducted in London have any chance of success and of rendering it easy for Austria to effect the indispensable compromise.

SAZONOV.

SECRET TELEGRAM FROM THE MINISTER FOR FOREIGN AFFAIRS TO THE MINISTER AT STOCKHOLM. DISPATCHED 19TH JULY, 1914. NO. 1603.

For your personal information. From a very reliable source we learn that the King informed the German Ambassador that in the event of a European war Sweden would range herself on the side of the Triple Alliance.

SAZONOV.

SECRET TELEGRAM FROM THE MINISTER FOR FOREIGN AFFAIRS TO THE AMBASSADOR IN MADRID. DISPATCHED 19/VII, 1914. NO. 1604.

In the event of the rupture of our diplomatic relations with Germany and Austria, please convey to the Spanish Government our request that their representatives in those countries should be instructed, in case of necessity, to take over the protection of Russian interests and the interests of Serbia which have been entrusted to us.

SAZONOV.

SECRET TELEGRAM FROM THE MINISTER FOR FOREIGN AFFAIRS TO THE AMBASSADOR IN VIENNA. DISPATCHED 19TH JULY, 1914. NO. 1622.

In the event of a rupture of relations between us and Austria also, you should proceed hither with the whole staff of the Embassy, after requesting your Spanish colleague to take over the charge of our interests in Austria-Hungary. Up to the present, however, we have not received any corresponding declaration from the Austrian Ambassador, and therefore we remain in diplomatic relations with Austria.

SECRET TELEGRAM FROM THE MINISTER FOR FOREIGN AFFAIRS TO THE AMBASSADOR IN VIENNA. DISPATCHED 20/VII, 2/VIII 1914. NO. 1624.

Please instruct Councillor of Embassy, Prince Kudashev, to come to St. Petersburg at once on matters of service.

SECRET TELEGRAM FROM THE MINISTER FOR FOREIGN AFFAIRS TO THE AMBASSADOR IN LONDON. COMMUNICATED TO PARIS 20TH JULY, 1914. NO. 1627.

Your telegram No. 226 received.

Germany is evidently endeavouring to transfer to us the responsibility for the rupture. Our general mobilization was called for because of the immense responsibility which would have fallen upon us if we had not adopted all possible precautionary measures at a time when Austria, while limiting herself to negotiations of a delaying character, bombarded Belgrade.

His Majesty bound himself by his word given to the German Emperor that he would not undertake any action of a provocative nature while negotiations with Austria continued. After such a guarantee, and after all the proofs of Russia's love of peace, Germany had no right to doubt our assurance that we would joyfully accept any peaceful issue compatible with the dignity and independence of Serbia. Any other issue would be quite incompatible with our own dignity, and would certainly shatter the European balance and establish the hegemony of Germany. This European, indeed world-wide, character of the conflict is infinitely more serious than its cause.

SAZONOV.

S. SVERBEEV'S NOTE (ORIGINAL TEXT).

De retour à Berlin mercredi le 16/29 Juillet 1914, j'allai voir l'Ambassadeur de France, M. Jules Cambon, qui me dit que la situation était, à son avis, des plus graves, et l'espoir d'une issue pacifique presque nul. Il ajouta que du moins, selon un télégramme de son frère, Paul Cambon, Ambassadeur de France à Londres, après le refus du Cabinet de Vienne d'accepter la réponse plus que conciliante de la Serbie à l'ultimatum Austro-Hongrois, l'appui effectif de l'Angleterre dans une guerre était assuré à la France et à la Russie.

Ayant vu le télégramme en question et ne le trouvant pas aussi persuasif que le prétendait mon Collègue de France, j'allai demander à Sir E. Goschen quelle était l'attitude de la Grande Bretagne dans la crise aigue que l'Europe était en train de traverser.

Ne recevant aucune réponse précise à ma question, j'expliquai mon point de vue à mon Collègue d'Angleterre et j'ajoutai, puisque l'Allemagne était persuadée que l'Angleterre garderait une stricte neutralité dans un conflit armé entre l'Allemagne et l'Autriche-Hongrie d'un côté et la Russie et la France de l'autre, *la clef de la situation se trouvait entièrement entre les mains de l'Angleterre.* Si Sir E. Grey n'hésitait pas *à déclarer nettement et catégoriquement* à Berlin que la Grande Bretagne était fermement décidée à marcher avec la Russie et la France, *la paix était assurée.* L'Ambassadeur d'Angleterre me répondit qu'il ne connaissait pas les intentions de son Gouvernement et, malgré tous les arguments que je produisai à l'appui de mon opinion, je ne reçus de sa part aucune réponse satisfaisante..

Ma première entrevue avec le Secrétaire d'Etat s'effectua à 5 heures de l'après midi. M. von Jagow me dit en me voyant entrer : " Les circonstances dans lesquelles nous nous retrouvons sont bien tristes," à quoi je répondis : " Vous les avez bien voulues."

Je répétai ensuite au Secrétaire d'Etat mon entretien avec M. Zimmermann, au lendemain du crime de Sarajévo, au cours duquel je lui avais fait observer que l'Autriche-Hongrie n'avait pas le droit de mettre au dos de toute la Serbie l'assassinat de l'Archiduc François-Ferdinand, assassinat qui avait été perpétré *en Autriche par un sujet Autrichien* ; que si le Cabinet de Vienne avait effectivement l'intention, ainsi que me le faisait comprendre M. Zimmermann, d'exiger que la Serbie ouvre une enquête afin d'établir les culpabilités de ceux de ses sujets qui avaient soi-disant participé à crime et de punir les coupables— s'il s'en trouvait—il devrait adresser cette *demande* non par une note officielle, mais en faire l'objet d'un entretien amical avec les Représentants du Royaume limitrophe, qui, je n'en doute pas et je n'hésite même pas à le certifier, se serait montré dans cette question de la correction la plus parfaite et cela d'autant plus, qu'il y allait de son propre intérêt—intérêt vital—de se mettre d'accord, après sa guerre victorieuse avec l'Autriche-Hongrie sur toutes les questions d'ordre économique qui liaient les deux états voisins.

Quant à l'ultimatum autrichien, continuai-je, il était inacceptable pour la Serbie, et l'Autriche-Hongrie le savait fort bien ; par conséquent elle voulait la guerre et elle savait de plus que la Russie ne pouvait rester indifférente à ce conflit armé. Ce qui m'étoune le plus, disai-je au Secrétaire d'Etat, c'est que l'Allemagne, connaissant cet ultimatum et sachant que nous ne pouvions admettre *ni l'écrasement ni l'affaiblissement* de la Serbie,—ait pu l'approuver : c'est qu'elle aussi, n'avait parait-il, rien contre la guerre.

M. von Jagow me répondit qu'il ne savait, soi-disant, rien de l'ultimatum et que d'ailleurs c'était une question qui touchait uniquement l'Autriche-Hongrie et la Serbie (la propagande serbe et l'assassinat de l'Archiduc). A quoi je m'écriai : " En ce cas Vous avez donné carte blanche à Votre Alliée."

Sans me donner de réponse à cette observation, le Secrétaire d'Etat me déclara que la Monarchie des Habsbourg ne voulait ui l'écrasement du Royaume limitrophe, ni d'annexions territoriales, mais qu'elle méditait simplement une expédition punitive. De plus, me dit-il, la Russie n'a rien à voir à la Serbie et lui, Jagow, n'admet pas le rôle de protecteur officiel que la Russie veut s'assumer dans les Balkans : " en ce cas l'Allemagne aurait tous les mêmes droits vis-à-vis des petits états protestants, comme par exemple, la Suède . . ." Il va sans dire que je protestai énergiquement contre cette argumentation qui *n'en était même pas une*; quant aux annexions territoriales, ajoutai-je, l'Autriche-Hongrie peut ne pas les vouloir en ce moment, mais je sais trop bien comment se font les guerres et qu'elles suites inattendues elles peuvent avoir. Je ne doute pas un moment que l'Autriche était quand-même fermement décidée à s'emparer du Sandjak, dont elle ne se pardonne pas jusqu'à présent la cession en 1898 (1908 ?)[1] pour mettre fin à la jonction de la Serbie avec le Monténégro.

Malgré que l'ultimatum Autrichien était inacceptable, continuai-je, la Serbie a cependant consenti à 8 ou 9 points, en étonnant l'Europe entière de sa conciliation. La monarchie des Habsbourg devait à son tour se contenter de cette réponse inespérée.

"Elle ne le pouvait," me répondit M. von Jagow, " parce que cette réponse était pleine de réticences, et les promesses qu'elle contenait n'étaient pas sincères." Je protestai énergiquement en observant qu'on n'avait pas le droit de douter de la sincérité de la Serbie.

Je passai là-dessus à la proposition de S. E. Grey que l'Allemagne avait refusée, proposition qui, sans être, peut-être, parfaite, était quand même une planche

[1] As written in the original.—ED.

de salut, car elle permettait de causer, tandis que les pourparlers entre les Cabinets que l'Allemagne avait proposés, étaient de beaucoup plus compliqués. Dans les moments aussi critiques que ceux que l'on traverse il faut profiter de chaque lueur d'espoir, car le temps presse et il s'agit de minutes et non pas de jours, ni même d'heures.

" Pas refusé," me répondit M. von Jagow, " mais trouvé pas pratique, les négociations du Cabinet à Cabinet l'étaient plus. D'ailleurs, ajouta-t-il, il n'était pas possible que 4 Grandes Puissances se constituent en aréopage pour juger les deux autres " ; à quoi je lui observai que l'une de ces Grandes Puissances, la Russie, y avait cependant consenti et que c'est encore l'Autriche-Hongrie qui avait refusé de participer à la conférence proposée par Grey, ne voulant pas comme toujours, faire de concessions. J'ajoutai que dans ces conditions la situation me paraissait être des plus graves et les suites grosses de dangers.

A ce moment on apporta à M. von Jagow une feuille de papier, qu'il me remit après l'avoir lue avec " consternation " en me demandant si la nouvelle qu'elle contenait était vraie : il s'agissait de notre mobilisation contre l'Autriche-Hongrie que j'étais chargé de lui communiquer. En lui confirmant cette nouvelle, j'appuyai, ainsi que j'étais chargé de le faire, que cette mesure n'avait *aucune pointe d'hostilité dirigée contre l'Allemagne*, et j'ajoutai que la mobilisation aux frontières de l'Autriche était d'autant plus motivée que la Monarchie des Habsbourg faisait elle-même, d'après des renseignements dignes de confiance qui m'étaient parvenus, de grands préparatifs militaires en Galicie.

En niant ces préparatifs M. von Jagow me dit, qu'après notre mobilisation contre l'Autriche-Hongrie, l'Allemagne était aussi obligée de mobiliser, qu'il n'y avait donc plus rien à faire et que les diplomates devaient céder dès ce moment la parole aux canons.

Je n'ai pas pu cacher à mon interlocuteur l'étonnement que me causait cette observation, car la veille encore il avait dit à Cambon que notre mobilisation contre l'Autriche n'aurait pas pour suite celle de l'Allemagne contre nous. M. von Jagow, très embarrassé me répondit : " Mais ayant appris que la Russie préparait ses troupes à la frontière de l'Allemagne, cette dernière était bien obligée de mobiliser de son côté."

Je lui observai que ce qui nous concernait nous, je n'en savait rien et je doutais que ces nouvelles fussent exactes quant à l'Allemagne je le savais pertinemment, d'après des renseignements dignes de foi, elle ne faisait que concentrer ses forces militaires contre nous.

M. von Jagow protestait énergiquement contre ces soi-disant préparatifs et tâcha, sans y réussir évidemment, de me persuader qu'on s'était borné à rappeler les officiers qui étaient en congé et les troupes qui avaient participé aux manœuvres. (L'occupation de Luxembourg par un corps d'armée de 100,000 hommes, au lendemain de la déclaration de la guerre par l'Allemagne est une preuve éclatante du contraire.)

Jeudi, 3 heures. Le *Local Anzeiger* anonnçait la mobilisation de l'Allemagne (mon télégramme chiffré).

3 heures 10. Démenti du bureau Wolff (mon télégramme au clair).

3 heures 15. Excuses et démenti von Jagow (mon second télégramme chiffré).

A 10 heures et demie du soir, n'ayant pas reçu le télégramme No. 2, contenant notre contreproposition à celle du Cabinet de Berlin, j'allai chez le Secrétaire d'Etat pour lui demander ce qu'il en savait.

M. von Jagow me dit avoir reçu un télégramme du comte de Pourtalès et après avoir parcouru ce long télégramme, il me lu le passage contenant le texte de la formule, que nous proposions,—texte qui correspondait à celui que je reçus le lendemain matin.

Je dis à Jagow que le Cabinet de Berlin devait accepter notre proposition qui était acceptable sous tous les points de vue et cela d'autant plus que la Serbie avait consenti à l'étonnement à 8 ou 9 points de l'ultimatum Austro-Hongrois.

Le Secrétaire d'Etat me répondit que c'était impossible et que la Monarchie des Habsbourg ne pouvait pas *s'humilier et porter un coup à son prestige.*

J'objectai que le prestige dune grande puissance ne pouvait pas être ébranlé par une concession de ce genre, que nous tâchions de toute manière de maintenir la paix, que l'Allemagne et l'Autriche-Hongrie ne voulaient, de leur côté, rien faire dans ce but et qu'après le bombardement de Belgrade qui était une satisfaction pour l'Autriche, cette dernière devait montrer plus de conciliation, j'ajoutais que la situation devenait *de plus en plus grave.* Tout ce que je disais à Jagow ne le fit pas changer de manière de voir.

Je repris cet entretien avec le Secrétaire d'Etat le lendemain, Vendredi, à 10 heures du matin enfaisant de mon mieux pour le convaincre d'accepter notre formule et d'agir sur le Cabinet de Vienne afin qu'il renonce à ceux des points de son ultimatum qui portaient atteinte à la souveraineté de la Serbie ; j'ajoutai que toute prolongation des pourparlers ne pouvant profiter qu'à l'Autriche, était *inadmissible* et que si, comme je le voyais, ni l'Allemagne ni son Alliée ne voulait faire de concessions (elles refusé) [1] la proposition de Grey et

---

[1] The word " ont " has evidently been omitted between these two words.—*Editor's note.*

l'Allemagne ne veut pas accepter notre formule, tandis que nous faisons tous nos efforts pour éviter une guerre européenne, *la guerre est inévitable.*

Je me butai à une obstination absolue du Secrétaire d'Etat, qui me donna la même réponse que la veille,— réponse qui me convainquait que toute négociation ultérieure était inutile.

A 2 heures de l'après midi M. von Jagow me pria de passer chez lui et me communiqua, sur un télégramme du Comt (?) Pourtalès, la nouvelle de notre mobilisation générale, en ajoutant *qu'après cela il n'y avait plus rien à faire,* que le Goûvernement Impérial et Royal était obligé de déclarer dès ce moment que la patrie était en danger et d'ordonner la mobilisation générale de l'Allemagne.

J'émis certains doutes sur l'authenticité de cette nouvelle (notre mobilisation générale), n'ayant aucune communication directe à ce sujet.

Jagow me reparla de l'échange de télégrammes de nos souverains, en me disant que l'Empereur Guillaume avait soi-disant accepté sur la demande de l'Empereur mon Auguste Maitre, le rôle de médiateur et qu'il avait même envoyé un télégramme à l'Empereur François Joseph : " Et c'est à ce moment là que Vous mobilisez toute Votre armée," me dit le Secrétaire d'Etat.

Je répondis, ainsi que je l'avais déjà fait précédemment, que l'échange des télégrammes entre Nos Souverains m'étant inconnu, je ne pouvais en parler ; que je voyais au contraire que l'Allemagne ne voulait rien faire pour la paix ;—quant au télégramme de l'Empereur Guillaume à l'Empereur François Joseph j'étais étonné que M. von Jagow ne m'en ait pas parlé avant et je le demandais si on en avait connaissance à St. Pétersbourg. Il me répondit qu'il "supposait"(?) que oui, et cela par un télégramme de l'Empereur Guillaume à l'Empereur mon Auguste Souverain.

(Le Secrétaire d'Etat me faisait comprendre durant tous nos entretiens précédents, que le Cabinet de Berlin ne pouvait user de son influence à Vienne dans le but d'incliner le Gouvernement Austro-Hongrois à des idées plus conciliantes.)

Au moment où je le quittais, M. von Jagow me répéta que la situation était sans espoir après notre mobilisation à quoi je répondis qu'étant optimiste de nature je ne disais jamais "fini" avant la fin, mais que franchement je ne voyais pas trop ce que l'on pouvait faire pour éviter la guerre.

A 3 heures entrée solenelle de l'Empereur Guillaume avec toute la famille Impériale à Berlin ; discours de Sa Majesté du Balcon, disant qu'on Lui imposait la guerre.

Le soir à 11 heures on m'apporta une feuille contenant l'ultimatum à la Russie—feuilles qu'on distribuait dans la rue.

Samedi, mobilisation générale Allemande (armée et flotte) et déclaration de la guerre à la Russie.

Dimanche matin à 10 heures et demie un employé du département des Affaires Etrangères m'apporta les passeports, en me disant que mon train se dirigeait sur Vergbolovo.

Dimanche matin à 11 heures—information que Sa Majesté l'Impératrice ne pouvait pas parvenir à Vergbolovo (?) et que mon train à moi prendrait aussi une autre direction,—laquelle on ne le savait pas encore.

Dans la journée—nouvelle de l'occupation du Luxembourg par un corps d'armée de 100,000 hommes

(8-ième corps) dont la mobilisation avait déjà été faite avant.

A partir du discours de l'Empereur Guillaume Vendredi 6 heures et quart p.m. toute négociation ultérieure était superflue.

(Signé) S. SVERBEEV.

APPENDIX II

Speeches of the Tzar and M. Poincaré on the 20th July, 1914.

(From Schulthess's *Europäischer Geschichtskalender*, München, 1917.)

At the banquet in the evening the Tzar proposed the following toast: " M. le Président ! Allow me to express to you how happy I am to welcome you here. The head of the friendly and allied State is always assured of the warmest reception in Russia. But our satisfaction in greeting the President of the French Republic is doubled to-day by the pleasure of finding in you an old acquaintance with whom I had the joy of entering into personal relationship two years ago. United since long ago by the mutual sympathy of their peoples and their common interests, France and Russia have been closely bound together during nearly a quarter of a century with the object of better pursuing one and the same aim, which consists in maintaining these interests by co-operating in the preservation of the balance and the peace of Europe. I do not doubt that both of our countries, true to their peaceful ideals and relying upon their proved alliance as also upon their common friendships, will continue to enjoy the benefits of the peace which the fullness of their strength ensures by constantly tying more tightly the bands which unite them. With this sincere wish I raise my glass to drink your health, M. le Président, and to the welfare and the glory of France."

M. Poincaré replied : " Sire ! I thank your Majesty for your hearty reception and beg you to believe that it has been a great pleasure to me to pay to-day another visit to the sublime Ruler of this friendly and allied nation. True to the path followed by my honourable predecessors, I have desired to bring to your Majesty here in Russia solemn evidence of the unalterable feelings dwelling in every French heart. Nearly twenty-five years have passed since our countries with clear vision have united the efforts of their diplomacy, and the happy effects of these enduring associations are daily made apparent in the world balance. Founded upon community of interests, consecrated by the peaceful desires of the two Governments, supported by armed forces on land and sea which know and value each other and have become accustomed to fraternize, strengthened by long experience and augmented by valuable friendships, the alliance to which the sublime Tzar Alexander III and the lamented President Carnot gave the initiative has ever since constantly afforded proof of its beneficial activity and its unshakable strength. Your Majesty can be assured that France in the future, as always in the past, will in sincere and daily co-operation with her ally pursue the work of peace and civilization for which both the Governments and both the peoples have never ceased to labour. I raise my glass in honour of your Majesty, of the Tzarina, of Her Majesty the Imperial Mother, of His Imperial Highness the Grand Duke, the heir to the Throne, and of the whole

Imperial Family, and I drink to the greatness and the welfare of Russia."

SPEECHES OF POINCARÉ AND THE TZAR ON THE 22ND OF JULY, 1914.

At the banquet on board the armed cruiser *France* the following toast was proposed by M. Poincaré: "Sire! I do not wish to leave this shore without once more declaring to your Majesty how deeply touched I am by the moving cordiality manifested towards me by your Majesty during my stay, and by the warm reception accorded to me by the Russian people. In these proofs of attention with which I have been overwhelmed, my country will see a new guarantee for the sentiments which your Majesty has always manifested towards France and an emphatic affirmation of the indissoluble alliance which unites Russia and my native France. With regard to all the problems which daily confront the two Governments and which demand the concerted activity of their united diplomats, there has always been agreement and always will be, and all the more readily because both countries have frequently experienced the advantages accruing to each from regular co-operation, and because they are both animated by the same ideal of peace combined with strength, honour and dignity. I drink to the welfare of your Majesties, of the Empress Maria Feodorovna, of His Imperial Highness the Grand Duke, the Heir Apparent, and the whole Imperial Family, and also to the fame of the Russian Empire."

The Tzar replied: "M. le Président! In thanking you for your amiable expressions, I particularly desire to say to you once more what great satisfaction we have derived from again having you with us. When you return to France I beg that you will convey to your beautiful country an expression of true friendship and hearty sympathy from all Russia. Our concerted diplomatic action and the brotherliness subsisting between our armed forces on land and sea will lighten the tasks of our respective Governments, whose duty it is to watch over the interests of our two allied peoples by working enthusiastically for the peace ideal which our nations, conscious of their strength, have adopted. On board of this fine ship bearing the renowned name *France*, I particularly desire to include the brave French Navy in the wish that I express as I raise my glass to your health, M. le Président, and to the fame and the welfare of France."

Sukhomlinov's "Recollections," Pages 364 and 365.

After the receipt of Kaiser Wilhelm's letter the further course of events was very greatly accelerated.

About midnight on the 16/29–17/30 of July the Tzar at Peterhof called me up on the telephone and acquainted me with the contents of a telegram he had received from Kaiser Wilhelm in which the latter begged the Tzar to stop our partial mobilization (*prekratit*), but said nothing about stopping the Austrian mobilization, and made me promise to bring influence upon the latter, which had been the first to have recourse to this step, to renounce it.

As I had not seen the Tzar since the 28th of July (see above), it can be understood that I was disturbed by this telephonic conversation. It was at once clear to me that the Tzar, trusting in the advice which he had allowed himself to receive behind the scenes, was wavering. If the Tzar had firmly decided to fulfil the desire of the German Kaiser, he would have had to give a direct order to stop the mobilization, but he failed to muster sufficient determination to come to such a decision. In my opinion this was not because such a decision would not be in accordance with the point of view of his trusted advisers, from whose influence he would willingly have freed himself, but which he was not able to shake off. In his situation between the hammer and the anvil the Tzar chose a middle course which enabled him, as he believed, to transfer the responsibility to other shoulders. He asks me : " Is it not possible to stop the mobilization ? " I reply by telephone that the mobilization is not a mechanical process which one can arrest at will, as one can a waggon, and then set in motion again. But with regard to the partial mobilization, if any order concerning it were issued I considered it my duty to report that subsequently much time would be necessary in which to re-establish the normal conditions for any further mobilization in the four districts affected. I therefore begged the Tzar, having regard to the importance of the matter, to call for another report concerning it from the Chief of the General Staff. That ended our conversation.

Some time later, during the night, Yanuschkevich called me up on the telephone and reported to me regarding a conversation he had had with the Tzar, to whom he had given a reply which agreed with what I also had reported to the Tzar. Therefore neither Yanuschkevich nor I received any order for the stopping of the partial mobilization, and we had no right to make any fresh arrangements concerning it, the less so because the partial mobilization against Austria was decided upon, not by the Tzar alone, but also by the Crown Council held on the 2nd of July. Under such circumstances Nicholas II found himself unable to cancel his own order without the co-operation of the Minister for Foreign Affairs, who had received his mandate from the Crown Council. The decision in this matter lay in the hands of the controller of our foreign policy and of those forces working behind the scenes which I was unable to control.

Extract from the book *Dokumente zur Kriegsschuldfrage*, vol. i. Telegraphic correspondence between Berlin and Petersburg during the July crisis in 1914. Translated from the *Red Archives*, vol. i, Historical Journal, Moscow, 1922. Published by the chief organization for investigating the causes of the war. Berlin, N.W. 6.

33. Secret Telegram from the Ambassador in Berlin, 16/29 July, 1914. No. 140.

Copy sent to Vienna.

No. 1539 received. During our friendly conversation the Minister endeavoured to convince me that Austria's assurance to the effect that she sought no territorial conquests, but only desired to give Serbia a lesson with regard to her provocative method of procedure, should serve as a basis for our compromise with Austria. The talk was then directed to the rumour concerning our partial mobilization, regarding which the Minister for Foreign Affairs apparently heard for the first time to-day by means of a brief report brought to him while I was present. After learning from me that we had really been obliged to mobilize the four military districts mentioned in your telegram, in informing him whereof I emphasized the fact that these measures were in no way directed against Germany, von Jagow replied in a highly excited manner that this unexpected news completely altered the situation and that he personally no longer saw any possibility of avoiding a European war. "If you mobilize against Austria you also . . .[1] measures against us." I sought to turn him from this opinion. "We are obliged to declare a mobilization against Russia, upon which mobilization against France will follow, and when all the Great Powers are under arms there seems to me no possibility of avoiding war." Hereupon I remarked that he had said to the French Ambassador that our mobilization on the Austrian frontier would not as yet render mobilization in Germany necessary, and this he could not deny, although he added that nevertheless the measures which we were adopting on the German frontier compelled Germany to think of her own protection. In his question as to whether Shebeko had been recalled, I replied in the negative. Towards the end of the conversation he read me a telegram from Pourtalès which had been brought to him wherein your conversation with Pourtalès regarding our partial mobilization was communicated. Jagow repeated that all that had been said here represented merely his personal view, and that therefore he would give me his final reply only after a discussion of the matter which he was about to have with the Chancellor. A ministerial council is summoned for this evening.

SVERBEEV.

(The above is not given in the Orange Book.)

[1] These periods indicate an omission.—*Note by German translator.*

46. SECRET TELEGRAM FROM THE AMBASSADOR IN BERLIN, 17/30 JULY, 1914. NO. 146.

Pressing. Instructions urgently requested. Copy to Vienna.

As up to then I had not received your telegram No. 2 with your proposals, I decided to go to the Minister for Foreign Affairs to ascertain what impression your proposal, founded upon Pourtalès's communication, had made upon him. The German Ambassador gives the following résumé of your proposal: " Austria recognizes that her conflict with Serbia affects European interests and declares herself ready to eliminate from her ultimatum those points which violate the sovereign rights of Serbia. In this event Russia engages to stop her military preparations." The Foreign Minister regards this proposal as unacceptable by Austria, as it would be humiliating for her and would lead to no favourable results. He added that, taken in connection with the news received concerning our mobilization against Austria, the situation had become worse and negotiations were becoming more difficult. The Minister for Foreign Affairs added despite this that Szapary had been instructed to continue negotiations with your Excellency, and that also a new proposal from Grey had come to hand which in all probability was already known in Petersburg. It must be remarked that after the bombardment of Belgrade, which according to Serbian reports was very . . . Austria, according to my view, might manifest a more yielding disposition.

SVERBEEV.

49. Secret Telegram from the Ambassador in Berlin, 18/31 July, 1914. No. 147.

Pressing.

Copy sent to Vienna.

The Minister for Foreign Affairs has just repeated to me [1] that the negotiations which had already been rendered difficult by our mobilization against Austria would become still more so in consequence of the serious military measures which we are taking against Germany. Information concerning these was coming in from all quarters and must call forth corresponding measures on the part of Germany. I replied that everybody arriving in Berlin [2] from the country testifies that also in Germany similar measures against us were in full progress. This was completely denied by the Minister for Foreign Affairs, who maintained [3] that here only officers who were on leave were being recalled and the troops which were engaged in manœuvres being sent back to their stations. I added that if in the present critical moment Germany and Austria for their part were not willing to manifest any goodwill in the matter of overcoming the crisis, a general collision was apparently inevitable. The Foreign Minister declared that Germany was making every effort to induce her ally to show moderation, and that he was at the moment impatiently awaiting information from Vienna as to how Grey's latest

[1] According to the Orange Book: "has just said to me."

[2] According to the Orange Book: "that according to trustworthy information received by me, which was confirmed by all country people arriving in Berlin," etc., etc.

[3] According to the Orange Book: "despite which the Minister for Foreign Affairs maintains," etc., etc.

proposal had been received there. I could not refrain from remarking to the Minister that the fact that neither the first English proposal nor ours of yesterday had met with any response in Vienna appeared to prove that the influence exerted in Vienna by Germany was insufficient. I found that generally speaking Jagow is in a very gloomy state of mind. He twice asked me whether Tatistchev, who up to now has not been present here, had returned.

SVERBEEV.

GEORGE ALLEN & UNWIN LTD
LONDON: 40 MUSEUM STREET, W.C.1
CAPE TOWN: 73 ST. GEORGE'S STREET
SYDNEY, N.S.W.: WYNWARD SQUARE
WELLINGTON, N.Z.: 4 WILLIS STREET

The League, the Protocol, and the Empire
By ROTH WILLIAMS
Author of "The League of Nations To-day"

Cr. 8vo.   5*s*.

"He argues fairly, convincingly, with restraint, and with great knowledge."—*Manchester Guardian*.

"A racy book. . . . Mr. Williams has a caustic wit, and his judgments are shrewd. . . . He is never dull, and is full of knowledge and resource."—*Foreign Affairs*.

What the League of Nations Is
By H. WILSON HARRIS

Cr. 8vo.   2*s*. 6*d*.

"A book for the ordinary man, who will find it as lively as it is informing. It is difficult to imagine anything better of its kind."—*Daily News*.

The World's Industrial Parliament
By E. M. OLIVER
Oxford University Extension Lecturer

La. Cr. 8vo.   2*s*.

"We can heartily commend it as a clear and succinct account of the achievements and possibilities of the International Labour Office."—*Manchester Guardian*.

International Social Progress
The Work of the International Labour Organization of the League of Nations
By G. A. JOHNSON

Demy 8vo.   10*s*. 6*d*.

"This is a valuable book. . . . Nothing so comprehensive has yet been attempted on so compact a scale."—*The Times*.

The Case for the Central Powers
An Impeachment of the Versailles Verdict
By Count MAX MONTGELAS
Translated by CONSTANCE VESEY

Demy 8vo.   10s. 6d.

"It fairly represents the strongest, clearest opposition which Allied defenders may expect to face. For that reason it ought to be read by all English students."—*Birmingham Post.*

The Limitations of Victory
By ALFRED FABRE-LUCE
Translated by CONSTANCE VESEY

Demy 8vo.   *About* 12s. 6d.

An impartial survey of the origins and immediate causes and lessons of the war, which acquires additional interest from the fact of its being the work of a Frenchman. M. Fabre-Luce deprecates the policy pursued by France since 1918, and would have his countrymen recognize that even victory has its limitations.

Isvolsky and the World War
By FRIEDRICH STIEVE
Translated by E. W. DICKES

Demy 8vo.   12s. 6d.

The author of this book prepared for publication for the German Foreign Office four volumes containing the diplomatic correspondence of Isvolsky, who was for some years the Russian Minister of Foreign Affairs, and was Ambassador in Paris during the critical years 1911–1914. In the present book Dr. Stieve states the conclusions which he draws from the correspondence, supporting them by copious extracts. The book develops a trenchant attack on the policy of Isvolsky and Sasonov and of M. Poincaré, all of whom it roundly charges with having worked for war.

The Neuroses of the Nations
The Neuroses of Germany and France before the War
By C. E. PLAYNE

Demy 8vo.   16*s.*

"A remarkable book. Shows not only profound thought, but clearness of vision and admirable powers of exposition."—*Foreign Affairs.*

The Geneva Protocol of 1924
By Sir JOHN F. WILLIAMS, K.C.B., C.B.E.

Demy 8vo.   1*s.*

"May be warmly recommended to all serious students."—*Manchester Guardian.*

A Short History of International Intercourse
By C. DELISLE BURNS

Cr. 8vo.   Second Impression,   Cloth, 5*s.*; Paper, 3*s.* 6*d.*

"A masterly little book. It deals with the Master-Key of the world's most urgent problem. . . . Its extraordinary lucidity makes it specially desirable for schools."—*Public Opinion.*

International Law
By CHARLES G. FENWICK

Medium 8vo.   21*s.*

"A useful restatement of principles."—*Law Journal.*
"The work is carefully annotated and well written."—*The Times.*

The Government of France

By JOSEPH BARTHÉLEMY

Translated by J. BAYARD MORRIS

Cr. 8vo.   *6s.*

"An exceedingly competent and convenient handbook on a subject of which the British public is strangely ignorant."—*Economist.*

Outlines of Polish History

By ROMAN DYBOSKI, Ph.D.

Professor of English Literature in the University of Cracow

Cr. 8vo.   *With a Map*   *7s. 6d.*

"A useful addition to our scanty literature on the subject. . . . As the work of a foreigner in English, it is a great achievement."—*Manchester Guardian.*

Builders of Peace

A History of the Union of Democratic Control

By Mrs. H. M. SWANWICK, M.A.

Foreword by the late E. D. MOREL, M.P.

Cr. 8vo.   *With Portraits*   *Cloth, 5s.; Paper, 2s. 6d.*

"This admirable book . . . should be read by everyone interested in international peace."—*Daily Herald.*

All prices are net

LONDON: GEORGE ALLEN & UNWIN LTD.
RUSKIN HOUSE, 40 MUSEUM STREET, W.C.1.

Form 45

940.9	R 924
Russia	

Form 47   940.9.   R 924

PENNSYLVANIA STATE LIBRARY
Harrisburg

In case of failure to return the books the borrower agrees to pay the original price of the same, or to replace them with other copies. The last borrower is held responsible for any mutilation.

Return this book on or before the last date stamped below.   21597

426	NOV 15 1967	
	MAR 20 1968	
DEC 18 1926	JAN -8 1969	
DEC '33		
Aug 20 '36		
Jun 5 '39		
Jun 25 43		
DEC